An old muskrat taught me a valuable lesson when I was 13. Cousins Bill and Rich Willis, my brother Larry and I had entered the muskrat and mink trapping business my parents had endorsed as an entrepreneurial endeavor. They wanted us to learn about business, be out in nature, and to catch the little pests that dammed up the creeks and flooded Willis farmland. Mink were scarce. Muskrats were plentiful. We placed simple traps in the swim-ways on the farms' ponds and caught the muskrat by their legs. Once or twice a day we checked traps and removed the wildlife. It was a great day if we caught five rats. We had to dispatch the semiaquatic rodents, rendering them breathless. None of us liked to skin and dry the hides, so we looked for someone experienced in processing fur. A Grass Lake schoolmate became another partner. He would share one fifth of the proceeds at the end of each year for skinning and aging the hides before we sold the fur.

Bill surprised us all with a humane way to kill the trapped muskrats during the second year of our business. We normally hit them on the back of the head with the blunt side of a hatchet. Bill's idea was to put them away using an 18-inch cord wrapped rapidly around the rodent's neck while the rat was still in the trap.

I am still not sure how Bill talked me into being the first to implement his plan, or why I didn't think it through. I guess I was young and naive. We arrived at the first trap with a live rat. He handed me the cord. I visually acted out the instructions and then went for the rat. The muskrat got me before I got him. Blood gushed from his bite on my right hand. Bill wrapped my palm in his red handkerchief and had me hold pressure on the wound as we drove to Dr. Faust's office. My four partners watched while the professional sewed me up. We all agreed ending a rat's life using the humane procedure was too risky. My business associates and I decided that sometimes the old tried and true ways were the best.

# TRANSACTION

*Exercising Long Term Business Strategies While Living a Balanced Life*

Phil Stephen Willis

Cover by RJMichaels
Layout by Angela Machnik
Consultation by Laurice Lazebnik


History, Michigan, Business, Entrepreneur

Printed in the United States of America

First Printing: September 2018
Amazon KDP

ISBN-978-0-692-08919-4

# PREFACE

You have probably heard about people learning things the hard way. Count me as one of them. I attribute much of my success in business to dogged persistence. Knowing what I am good at doing is key to that success. That focus is my accounting business. My firm is the Golden Goose that produces the golden eggs that has supported me through the decades. I have stretched my wings and taken risks investing in different industries, but I always come back to doing what I do best.

I contribute much of my success in life to being involved, open and attentive to opportunity. Like everyone else I have faced personal tragedy. I have learned to make opportunities out of problems by using the lessons my parents taught me, common sense principles I still use every day in my professional life

My wife, Pat, and I believe in keeping a balance between business and pleasure. Many people today put in long hours. Vacations seem to be rare, guilty pleasures. We have each learned that we can bring more to our work desks if we take time out to recharge our batteries. We look for activities that we love that are separate from work. Rewarding ourselves seems to energize the next big deal or the next great quest. I love sports, boating, hunting, and nature. We invest in our joy, in our health, and in the quality of our lives. Both Pat and I love what we do. Retirement is a distant thought. We have been rewarded with good friends and family. We remain involved with our community. Neither of us will have regrets at the end of our lives that we didn't do things we always wanted to do. We generally do them.

## Table of Contents

# CHAPTER 1

## *Turning Problems into*
## *Opportunities*

Building long-term success did not come easily for me. It took careful planning and perseverance. I have found that successful projects easily attained usually do not last.

It takes good health, too; mental and physical. I begin each morning committed to being the best that I can be. During my 40-minute morning workout I fine-tune my daily "to do" list placing the most important and difficult tasks at the top, then hit the road running with communications flying on my way to work. I get there by 7:30 am.

The list stems from work efforts of the prior few days and rarely stops evolving during the day. The agenda includes planning for vacations and weekends. Tough tasks get tackled early. Problems get solved, new ideas emerge, and opportunities float to the surface becoming the foundation for tomorrow's list. I am not looking to fix short-term problems but to set in place building blocks for long-term, lasting solutions.

For instance, Pat and I were enjoying one of our long-term goals on the Intercostal Waterway on the east coast of Florida. We were reaping the results of our hard work and investments, soaking up sunshine on the bridge of our 53 foot ocean-going vessel, *TransAction*. Pat and I love boating. It takes every bit of our focus leaving no room for distractions from the workplace. Boating fills our days with adventure.

I was concentrating on piloting the vessel and Pat was watching the GPS and channel markers when an unexpected movement in the water presented a new challenge for both of us. The fishing boat we were following suddenly veered to the wrong side of the channel markers. We had prepared for this boating adventure. We had studied about the positioning of waterway warnings during Power Boat Training on Michigan's Great Lakes.

The fishing boat captain, I concluded, had made a mistake. So, I continued to keep the green markers on the starboard side of our new vessel. Wrong. Almost instantly, we ran onto a sand bar. I was surprised to see the fishing boat continue forward while we sat there, beached on the bottom. Today's boating adventure had turned into a boating challenge.

Life, it seems to me, is a series of sandbars. I have spent most of my personal and professional life analyzing problems and identifying the challenges ahead. I look at the positive side of each situation and pursue it surrounded by a team of happy, positive professionals. I transact business every day, overcoming obstacles that stand in the way of our client's success and then turn their business challenges into opportunities. That is what I do. I am a CPA, a Certified Public Accountant. I work in Jackson, Michigan. I should be able to get this boat out of the mud.

# CHAPTER 2:

## *"Whistlestop, Grass Lake*
## *Railroad Depot"*

I was born right after the Great Depression in 1941 near a typical Midwestern small town. During this economic downturn anyone who had debt was sunk. If a family could not pay what they owed they lost everything. My folks were prepared for the Depression. We lived with the attitude that we had to save, waste nothing, work hard and minimize debt. I did not grow up on Wall Street and our farmhouse outside of Grass Lake, Michigan was not a palace, but that experience gave me an education in finance and work ethic.

My brother and I learned physical work was part of a healthy lifestyle. Back then lifting hay bales and shoveling manure was as normal a part of my day as eating and sleeping. Coaches recruited farm boys for their football teams because we were usually in better shape than city boys.

Now I pull weeds around our home to keep in shape. Pat and I live on a lake near Jackson not far from my ancestral homestead. I do not have to go to the gym for a workout. Yard work can be my exercise. For many years at the large office building we owned I shoveled, swept the walk, and used the leaf blower to clean the parking area instead of sitting at my desk all day. I found it was a good time to clear my mind, get away from the office and computers. Physical work has always been and still is an opportunity for me to dream and think of new ideas for clients and my community.

An arsonist set fire to the historic train station in my hometown in 1980. The flames left only the rock walls surrounding the Grass Lake depot where my grandfather worked. Architecture in small towns preserves the character and charm of a community. Now we were left with a burned-out eyesore and a hole in our history.

The Central Railroad, which later became the Michigan Central Railroad or MCRR, laid tracks in 1842 through what we now know as the Village of Grass Lake. At that time the price of land at the former village center was $2 an acre. A resident who owned property about a mile and a half from the town center offered his land for $1.50 per acre. The track was laid through the low bidder's property and the first depot was built next to the track. The building was a simple wooden structure. Several businesses from the old village center were moved to the new location to be within an easy walk to the new train line.

Ann Arbor, a city 30 miles east of Grass Lake, was awarded a new stone depot in 1887 by the MCRR. The architects were Spier and Rohns, a Detroit firm. That depot today is the Gandy Dancer, a fine restaurant.

Grass Lake was offered a smaller version of the stone depot to replace their existing 50-year-old wooden structure. Both railroad stations were built in what was known as the Richardsonian Romanesque Revival design.

Back then, mail was sorted on the train and delivered to depots along the track for distribution. Each railroad terminal also contained a telegraph office. Stones for both buildings were mined from Foster's Station, a quarry northwest of Ann Arbor. The massive stone structures, solid in appearance, were intended to inspire trust in the services of Michigan Central. The growth of Grass Lake centered on this new stone structure.

# CHAPTER 3:

## *A Community Dream*

The depot ruins sat vacant for years after the fire of 1980. I credit a community group for trying to buy and rebuild the ruined landmark. The owner at that time, James Leonard, would not sell the property even though numerous offers were made. Finally, the Village Council had the depot and an adjoining gas station, also owned by Leonard, condemned and ordered to be torn down. That's when I got involved.

I just could not imagine the village without that historic railroad depot. My grandfather, Phil Sheridan Willis, had served as the ticket agent in that stone building for three years in the late 19th century. I was certain that restoring the terminal for community functions would have the added value of stimulating the redevelopment of downtown Grass Lake, a village that had suffered after the destructive fire.

Talks began with Leonard. He agreed to accept our offer of $65,000 in 1988 but delayed drawing up the documents until the Village threatened demolition. The building remains were unsafe and an ugly scar on Grass Lake's main street.

I was in shock when my friend and local building contractor, Michael McKay, called to tell me he and James Mitchell had purchased the depot and adjoining property to build a Shell gas station and convenience store. He said they planned to restore the depot to house Mitchell's Lionel train collection. The depot would be used for private purposes. When I recovered my ability to speak, I asked for a meeting with the two men. I explained the desire of local citizens to purchase the depot and our efforts to keep it a public building, available to area residents for special events. We talked several times over the next 30 days.

The Whistlestop Park Association was formed and incorporated as a result of those talks. We chose the name Whistlestop after the novel *Whistle Stop*, written by Jackson native Maritta Wolff. The 1941 novel was about small-town Midwestern life in post-Depression America. A former resident of Grass Lake, she had based her book loosely on our town and had received a favorable review in the *New York Times*.

McKay and Mitchell had a change of heart and sold the property to our non-profit organization for the same amount they paid for it, $75,000. They even agreed to make a substantial cash donation to our newly formed tax-exempt organization. The association took out a loan to pay for the property and we applied for and received a grant from the state of Michigan to restore the depot and adjoining park. That was a huge victory, but it was only the beginning. Volunteers worked to restore the depot and the surrounding property for the next three and a half years.

My Grandfather

Sarah Taylor Willis

My Grandmother

# CHAPTER 4:

## *Implementing the Dream*

I knew we had to get the community involved. I contributed seed money to motivate investors and lead by example. We started by recruiting a small core of stakeholders with influence in the village to get the project locked in. Al Molenkoft, the supervisor of Grass Lake Township at the time, was a leading volunteer and cheerleader.

We promoted the first local fund-raising event, a kick-off dinner with keynote speaker Neale Shine of the *Detroit Free Press*. Neale was known for his historic preservation efforts in the Detroit area. U.S. Senator Nick Smith attended. We raised a few thousand dollars from the 125 people attending and identified some guests as potential leaders for the project.

We held another community event which featured live and silent auctions on Michigan Avenue in front of the depot ruins. Newspaper coverage added attention to our cause. Our volunteers solicited more donations and recruited even more help.

Publicity grew but even with all the promotion there were many resident disbelievers who turned down our requests for help. We continued raising money and were awarded two state historic restoration grants.

Overall progress was slow. Skeptics watched as large fieldstones, taken from the Taylor/Willis farmland were restored or replaced on the building's exterior. People stared as local building contractors volunteered their services and free materials. They gawked as volunteers from the county bricklayers' union restored the brick walls and walkways with original bricks from the 1887 construction. New volunteers joined in the efforts as the longtime doubters stood by and watched the progress.

The big question was when and how the ornate roof would be constructed. Members of the Whistlestop Park Association were determined to duplicate the 1887 style of the original contoured roof. This unique design would be an expensive project. We had professionally drawn blueprints produced for historical accuracy but most builders would not touch the roof project. Very little progress was accomplished over the next six months while we recruited more help and money. And then Richard Clark, a local contractor, came forward and offered to build the complicated roof at a discounted rate.

Disbelievers became believers when the trusses were installed on the newly resurrected depot. Cynics were now anxious to claim their part as the community gained confidence the project would be completed. The Grass Lake Depot was rededicated in September 1992.

Maritta Wollf attended to help us celebrate. She even signed my copy of her book.

The Whistlestop Park Association and the Grass Lake Depot continue to serve as a community event venue. Graduations, weddings, showers, luncheons, parties, and other family events use this historic and beautiful location.

Not long ago some of Grass Lake High School's fifth-generation Willis children invited Pat and me to attend their pre-prom night party for pictures. We asked where it would be held and were told, "At the Depot," like we should know where the cool place was. We have attended many events at the train depot, but this one created a traffic gridlock at Grass Lake's historic town center. The depot was the cool place to be.

Partnerships, volunteerism, and community involvement had moved boulders to rebuild this edifice where our grandkids and their friends and families now played. That night when Pat and I attended the children's event it was hard to keep tears from forming. Our team had overcome the odds. We had persevered. All our efforts were worth it! Take strength from this story and never give up on your dreams.

Whistlestop Depot – March 2018

# CHAPTER 5:

## *Loving Nature*

It was important to my parents that their children learn to respect nature and the land, so when my young brother, Larry, and I developed an interest in birds, Mom and Dad presented us with a unique Christmas present. I was about five at the time. The combination bird book, two ten-inch, 78-rpm records, and portable record player were my all-time favorite childhood gifts. They allowed my brother and me to identify various types of birds.

"Bozo and the Birds" featured Bozo, a clown who appeared on TV in 1949 along with his pogo stick. We eagerly turned to page one of the new book and started our record player. The recording began with a jovial voice saying, "Hi, I am Bozo the Clown. I will take you around the world on my pogo stick and introduce you to many of my bird friends." When it was time to turn the page, the record made a "boing" sound and a voice said, "Turn the page."

"Ho, ho, ho," Bozo would say. "We have landed by a kingfisher that lives on the bank of a stream. The kingfisher dives in the water for fish. Well, we had better be going." Bozo would boing on his pogo stick and it was time to turn the page again. The next page displayed an unusual spoonbill bird that looked like a flamingo standing by Bozo and his pogo stick. "Bozo has now landed by a duck-billed platypus who feeds under the water on the fresh growing water plants." And the story would go on.

Larry and I read and played that Bozo book hundreds of times. We memorized the words and later learned to read them. I never tired of this educational tool. The portable record player was high technology in 1949. TV, video games, and cell phones had not yet been invented. Outside of reading books and playing family board games, listening to records was our entertainment.

Bozo inspired my adult travels and piqued my curiosity for birds, for identifying animals, and for the strong urge for adventure. I remember the excitement of spotting a spoonbill on one of our boat trips in the Florida Everglades, a bird I recognized from Bozo's book.

My favorite outdoor observation point as a child was the window in the living room of our farmhouse on Willis Road. It had a southern exposure. The back of the couch was pushed against the window and provided me a view of a large mowed lawn, a variety of trees, and a circular drive. I began feeding the birds in the flower box attached to the house directly under the window. Sunflower seeds became their favorite. When I came home from school, my job was to resupply the flower box. Then I could proceed to my observation point and on any given day see chickadees, nuthatches, cardinals, finches, and blue jays.

Before I was 12 I ran farm equipment in the field by myself. I mowed hay and raked it into rows for chopping or baling with our International Farmall Super C tractor. Farm kids could get permits to drive cars at 14. The hard work started during the harvest. We stacked bales of hay onto wagons by hand and then unloaded them onto long conveyers called elevators that carried them into the barn. The most difficult job was stacking the 40 to 50-pound bales inside the barn where temperatures could reach 100 degrees. Moving hundreds of bales was a body builder and prepared us for football in the fall, a silver lining to a sweaty job.

One afternoon while mowing hay near a pond on the northeast corner of the farm a mature Sandhill crane ran in the hay in front of the mower. Mature cranes stand almost four-feet high and were extremely rare in our area. I glanced back. My mower's blades were crushing a baby crane. I was devastated. The baby had been hiding in the 18-inch hay. That experience has weighed heavily on my mind and reminds me of the importance of protecting endangered species.

Today I work at improving wildlife habitat with DUCKS Unlimited, Pheasants Forever and Michigan Whitetails Unlimited. Instead of selling off Willis land to developers or clearing it for additional farmland, we work with the Crop Reserve Program of the United States Department of Agriculture. We have pulled 35 acres of land out of cultivation for ten years for all kinds of wildlife habitat.

Me in the "Man-Cave" at the Willis Farm

# CHAPTER 6:

## *The Family Vacation*

My first travel adventure was a road trip in a 1952 Pontiac Dad borrowed from the company inventory at Grass Lake Implement. Mother had games to entertain Larry and me, preserve the new upholstery and keep us quiet as we headed south on US-127 for the three-day drive to Florida.

My father was familiar with Lake Mary, Ohio, a primary staging area for ducks and geese migrating to the northern states and Canada. We landed there on our first day out. Thousands of birds bobbed on the waters as Dad explained their flyway to us. It was the same air corridor their ancestors had flown for decades. He said the birds feeding in the adjoining fields were impatiently waiting for the snowmelt and the weather to warm in Michigan before making the next leg of their flight north.

Dad was as determined to migrate as the ducks were, but he wanted to move in the opposite direction and get to Florida in three days, so he did most of the driving. Mother occasionally took the wheel to give him a break.

Since there were no fast food restaurants back then, Mother packed lunches that we ate in the car. We stopped only for gas or restroom breaks.

Father pulled into a motel in Berea, Kentucky at dusk, our planned stop. We were all tired. He came out of the office shaking his head. The rate was too high. Dad was never opposed to adjusting his plans if the reasons were valid. We drove on looking for a vacant sign on another motel. He reappeared after the next stop with a smile and said, "Unload the car." Dad told us they wanted $18 a night, but he had negotiated the rate to $15. "Not bad for four people with a bath and shower!" He was beaming.

I learned from my dad to be frugal and to negotiate. Larry did too. My brother shared Dad's lessons later in life with his family. He and his wife Barb enjoyed life and had many friends. Barb told me this story about friends from Grand Rapids on a trip to Disney World.

She, Larry and children Kelly & Myk drove an old Econoline van. Their friends drove a fancy new van. Larry & Barb rented one room for their family of four. The other couple rented two rooms. Barb said her family shared restaurant meals with little or no waste. The other couple let their children order whatever they wanted rarely finishing a meal. Barb said she packed meals for some of their activities while the other family made stops to purchase whatever they wanted. Barb and Larry's children grumbled in vain about the extravagances of the others. The two families had fun together and equally enjoyed the educational experiences and relationship building that came with their travels.

Barb and Larry continued to accumulate assets over the years, a vacation home on Lake Michigan, a larger home on the Thornapple River in Ada, and a favorite car to drive in each season of the year. The years flew by. Their children completed their college education debt free. Larry & Barb were able to enjoy a similar lifestyle to the other family.

A few years later the other couple called on Barb at her retirement condo in Florida. Their condo was "underwater." It had more debt than value and the payments were more than their cash flow. They were being evicted with no place to go. Barb, a kind and considerate person, agreed to refinance the condo for her old friends with reduced payments, permitting them to keep their home.

This story is about two different financial lifestyles, one planning with the long-term in mind, the other with immediate gratification. Long-term financial conservatism in a business works the same way. I have seen the demise of many firms when owners take out too much in wages and benefits. They leave no money in the business for buying power and future opportunities. I have learned in my business ventures that future financial rewards happen when I exercise patience, perseverance, and sacrifice in a company's early years. Fast roads to success are rare and usually rife with hazards.

There were no expressways in the days of our first family trip, so my dad drove slowly through each town and city. Larry and I learned patience on the long ride, while my folks persevered.

We followed Dad's plan for day three and stopped to see my sister, Marilyn Willis Ouellette and her family in Augusta. My folks were anxious to meet their new grandchild. Both Dick and my sister worked as teachers after he got out of the service. I remember their third-floor apartment as being hot. It had two small windows, no air-conditioning, and old appliances that she served hot dogs from every night for a week. During our stay in Georgia Dad was able to influence their decision to move back to Michigan where Dick got a job teaching in Addison, not far from Grass Lake.

We left Georgia for Bradenton, Florida to visit Glen Harshbarger, a neighbor and farmer from Grass Lake. Glen invited us to go fishing for Snook. Trolling down the river in a 12-foot aluminum fishing boat, Glen instructed Larry and me to keep our eyes focused on the north shore. He said we would see something big. And we did. A giant alligator about the size of our boat was sunning on the south bank. We huddled near our dad in the center of the boat and peeked around him. We watched the gator enter the water as our boat approached. We were ready to forget the Snook, get off that river, and head back to the safety of Grass Lake.

We left Bradenton on Highway 41 for Seminole Indian Territory, my parent's planned lesson for the day. We were to learn why the highway was called Alligator

Alley. We had already learned to respect what was under the water from Mr. Harshbarger's river ride. Now we would learn what could be waiting for us on shore. We motored by a few small villages where the natives appeared to live like they had for hundreds of years, surviving off the surrounding lands and tourism traffic. My father stopped at one village that offered woven products. They also had large pens filled with alligators. Larry and I revved up our courage to peek over the walls. We were eager to move on after snapping a few quick photos.

That trip fueled a desire in me for more travel adventures. When my sons were young we enjoyed snowmobiling at the Willis farm in Grass Lake, and in Northern Michigan where we also dipped smelt during the season. My then wife, Carolyn, and I planned trips with the boys to Lake Bellaire and went snow skiing at Schuss Mountain. We enjoyed many wonderful trips to Cedarville in the U.P. with Phil, Barb and Todd Marston. Barb is Carolyn's sister. We drove our motor home to Disney World, to Gettysburg and on to Washington D.C. We even toured the White House.

But even well-planned family vacations can be scuttled by the unexpected. I had noticed a chain of lakes in Northern Michigan on my map that carried on for nearly a hundred miles. It reminded me of the Wolf Lake series of lakes I loved to boat in my youth. It was maybe seven miles long. This Northern Michigan train of lakes was 10 times the size with unlimited opportunities for new adventures.

In 1979 my wife, two sons and I towed our Ski Nautique behind our motor home for a well-deserved family week up north. The plan was a good one. We would stop at my brother Larry's in Grand Haven for a family reunion and some water skiing, and then proceed north for a week of adventure at a rental cottage near Torch Lake.

The adventure stalled after water skiing with Larry's family on Lake Michigan. We broke the propeller when it hit sandbags as we were taking the boat out. The obstructions had been placed in Lake Michigan to protect the shoreline from erosion. It took the entire next vacation day to find a shop to repair the prop.

When we finally reached our rental cabin, it was not up to my family's expectations. We made it work. It was a vacation, after all. Smiles returned when we launched the Ski Nautique on Elk Lake. But then the starter on the boat's motor gave me trouble. I got it going and told my crew we could ski as long as no one turned off the key. Skiing proved great through Elk Lake and on into Torch Lake until somehow the boat stalled mid-lake.

Frustrated, I howled, "Who turned off the motor?" No one would admit to the deed. We floated on Torch Lake in silence while I fiddled with the starter. We waived down a passing boat for a tow to the closest marina, 10 miles away from our launch site. At this point my wife was madder than a hornet. She dug in her heels when we arrived at the marina and refused to leave.

While making arrangements for a loaner car, I explained to the owner that I would drive it to the Elk Lake launch to retrieve our motorhome. Scott would return the car to the marina and I would drive the motorhome and trailer. The owner of the car said, "Does this boy have a drivers license?" Scott was 13, but looked older. We loaded the boat on the trailer, and returned to the second-rate rental cottage late that night.

We toured the area for the next couple of days, but the weather was as lousy as our moods. Our family vacation ended early the next day when we all decided to head south for home.

# CHAPTER 7:

## *Looking Back as a Road Forward*

Turning problems into opportunities is how I like to live. As I stood there that day in Florida at the helm of *TransAction* wondering how I would maneuver that vessel off the bottom, my memory floated back to 1951. I thought about the lessons I learned on the farm from my father before he died. It was advice I have shared with family and clients during my career as an accountant, useful advice about planning and preparation.

I was about four when I volunteered to work in the barn with our hired hand, Millard Hashley. Dairy cows were held in stanchions for the entire winter. It was rare they got outside the building until spring. Their feed was brought to them and their waste carried away. Farmhands used wide shovels to scoop the sloppy, stinky mess into wheelbarrows. The single-wheeled transports were pushed up a plank, their contents dumped into a manure spreader, and this natural fertilizer was spread across the fields.

I asked Mr. Hashley if I could help him clean the brown stuff out of the gutters and wheel it up the plank into the manure spreader. I was wearing my brand-new red snowsuit that day. While he thought about it, I asked permission to climb to the top of the plank that was leaning on the edge of the spreader. It was about four feet off the ground. Millard nodded. I walked to the top, looked down and remember being thrilled to be standing so high up.

Millard said he needed to move it and politely asked me to come down. I demanded, as four-year olds can do, that I remain standing at the top while he moved the bottom. As soon as he moved the board, I slipped, hit my head on the rail of the spreader and fell headfirst into the manure. Millard pulled me out and tried to clean the muck from my new, red snowsuit, but when he saw I was bleeding from my forehead, our hired hand carried me into the farmhouse.

Mother drove me to Dr. Faust in downtown Grass Lake. I remember sitting in the waiting room with her holding Millard's red handkerchief to my forehead while we waited for the doctor to clean the wound and stitch me up. She told him I had been working on our farm when the accident occurred but had not followed the directions of our hired hand. That was the first of many visits I would make to that examination room during my early years. I imagine the charge was less than five dollars in those days.

The gash healed well, but a few years later when I noticed a dent in my forehead, I learned my skull had been fractured and that I probably had a concussion. I look back and think that Mother Nature and the Lord have magnificent healing powers. Some people tease me today and say my thought processes are the result of hitting my head on the rail of that manure spreader.

Work assignments changed throughout my adolescence. During my teen years I was given the privilege of driving the tractor to spread the manure. Millard Hashley never bothered to warn me not to spread manure downwind. It took me one windy day to realize and learn from that mistake.

My most useful lesson on that farm happened when I was ten. Dad and my Uncles Dean and Gale had arrived at our family home in Grass Lake with a Chinese pheasant and several species of duck from their day of hunting. While the wild game was cleaned and carefully prepared for our family meal, Dad had my brother Larry and I join our uncles outside for target practice.

Handling a gun safely was a high priority with my dad. He knew in a few years we would want our own hunting rifles. While he and my uncles took turns shooting, Dad explained what every hunter should know. He taught us never to point a loaded or unloaded gun at anything unless we intended to use it. The second lesson, and the more useful one had much broader implications for his sons who would both become Certified Public Accounts. Dad drummed into us that a successful hunter prepares for the hunt and plans his shot before he shoots.

The targets that evening were clay pigeons. The men had constructed and tested a sheet metal barricade that could withstand any type of fired shotgun shell and protect the operators of the pigeon thrower. My brother Larry and I were to be the operators. This spring-loaded devise discharged four-inch clay discs into the air at lightning speed at a variety of angles and heights. Dad explained he used shotgun pellets because the shell's range was a hundred feet and the pellets could fan out and hit the fast-moving water birds he would be hunting.

Our job, after we loaded the thrower, was to say "ready," and then wait for him to yell "pull." That is when we discharged the clay discs. The clay pigeons flew from the barricade for a hundred feet and were a simulation of a duck or pheasant taking flight. The dads shot several 25-unit boxes of 12-gauge shells filled with pellets. When there was a break in the action, my brother and I gathered the spent shell casings. I remember enjoying the acrid scent of burnt gunpowder. Then we went inside and devoured the game birds Mother had so lovingly prepared.

I was eleven when I was invited to join in the target shooting. The first time I carried my own gun was in the fall of 1952. The plan was for Dad, Larry and me to leave the house in the early morning dark to hunt ducks behind Aunt Esther's farm at 2332 Willis Road. This shallow, two-acre pond with two islands in the center has been the premier duck-hunting hole for our family for six generations. Dad reminded us a successful duck hunter was a quiet and patient duck hunter. He said the pursuit of wild game was a lot like every other challenge we would face in our lives. "Remember boys, never aim a gun at anything you don't want to shoot." We followed Dad's plan and entered the marsh from the south. I stationed myself in the tall grass before sunrise. Larry was still too young to carry a gun, so he stayed beside Dad.

The fall colors on the maples, hickory, and oaks glowed as the first rays of light broke through woods. I could hear the water birds quacking. Sunrise exposed the clutch of ducks on the far side of the pond well out of my range. A short time later the birds took flight. A flock of seven mallards set down on the pond in front of Dad and Larry. I was about 50 feet to the west of them. It was clearly Dad's shot. I didn't stand or raise the gun butt to my shoulder, but I was prepared. My gun was loaded. My finger was on the safety. I was alert. I waited. I watched Dad stand and fire two rounds. I watched my father miss his target.

The flock turned in front of Dad and Larry and flew toward me. I stood, and with thoughtful precision planted my feet and aimed my 12-gauge double-barreled shotgun. I touched the trigger. The gun butt rammed against my shoulder. Fire shot from the barrel. The blast echoed back to me across the pond. I was dazed when the single drake dropped into the water not far from where I stood. It took a moment before I realized I had bagged my first mallard duck. I was unable to move.

Dad approached me in his waders, a wide grin on his face. "Nice shot," he said. He slogged out to retrieve the duck and handed me the bird to carry to the farmhouse. Dad's hand was on my shoulder as he reported my success to mother who we found working in the kitchen. I am confident my love for the outdoors and hunting grew out of that moment.

Good planning and preparation were not the only lessons I learned in that pond behind Aunt Esther's. When Mother thanked me for providing food for the table that evening, it was the first time I felt pride at being able to contribute to my family through my efforts. The duck tasted fantastic at dinner that night.

Phil Sterling Willis II, My Father

# CHAPTER 8:

## *Entrepreneurs in the Making*

New projects or adventures usually work when I remember my father's lessons to research, prepare and plan before venturing out. We used them preparing for this boating adventure on the Intercostal Waterway in Florida. Pat and I had studied the charts and planned routes carefully for months before our trip. We took a couple half-day Power Squadron boat safety classes offered by the U.S. Coast Guard. Besides prepping us for years of enjoyment on the water, those classes also qualified us for discounts on our boater insurance, a silver lining that's always there if we look for it.

This ten-day boating adventure would have been considered overly ambitious even for experienced Florida mariners. My sister Marilyn spends winters in Florida and is familiar with the unpredictable weather and concealed coral reefs. When she heard our plans, she said we were crazy. My mother met us at the airport already apprehensive about the length of our proposed trip.

We left the boat slip at her Highland Beach condo early New Year's Day of 1997. *TransAction* motored north to Stuart on Florida's Intercostal Waterway on the first day of our adventure. I remember feeling my heart rate increase as my adrenalin pumped. Our plan was to meet friends from Jackson in Stuart and watch the Rose Bowl game together. The trip would not have been far by car, but when cruising no-wake zones on the canal and waiting for bridges to open, it can take hours, and it did.

We followed vessels with Florida registrations up the waterway. Local boaters helped us identify bridge names and times of operation. We were progressing well as we headed around Peanut Island at West Palm Beach. Pat watched for markers and checked the charts as I followed her directions and crosschecked them on the Global Positioning System screen. The red triangle markers were all on the port, the left, and the green square markers were on the starboard. It seemed remarkably easy as we made our way north. But that's when we beached *TransAction*.

Boats motored by as we sat there weighing our options. We could back her off the sandbar, if it was a sandbar, but the props, drive shafts, and rudders might be damaged if it was another obstruction. We were clearly novices in this situation. My hands gripped the wheel. I noticed the muskrat scar. That critter taught me a valuable life lesson when I was 13. The teeth marks that muskrat left me with have been a useful reminder over the years to trust the wisdom of professionals.

None of us had much wisdom when we were teenagers. Cousins Bill and Rich Willis, my brother Larry and I had entered the muskrat and mink trapping business my parents had endorsed as an entrepreneurial endeavor. They wanted us to learn about business, to be out in nature, and to figure out how to catch the little pests that dammed up the creeks and flooded Willis farmland. We soon learned that mink were scarce and muskrats were plentiful. The partners placed simple traps in the swim-ways on the farms' ponds and caught the muskrat by their legs. Once or twice a day we took turns checking the traps and removing the wildlife. It was a great day if we caught five rats. We'd skin them at home, using precut shingles to stretch, age and dry the skins before selling the fur.

It was our job to dispatch the semiaquatic North American rodents, rendering them breathless. None of us liked to skin and dry the hides, so we looked for someone experienced in processing fur. A Grass Lake schoolmate became another partner. He would share one fifth of the proceeds at the end of each year for skinning and aging the hides.

Cousin Bill surprised us with a humane way to kill the trapped muskrats during the second year of our business. We normally hit them on the back of the skull with the blunt side of a hatchet. Bill's idea was to put them away using an 18-inch cord wrapped rapidly around the rodent's neck while the rat was still in the trap.

I am still not sure how Bill talked me into being the first to implement his plan, or why I didn't think it through. I guess I was young and stupid. We arrived at the first trap with a live rat and he handed me the cord.

I visually acted out his instructions and went for the rat. The muskrat got me before I got him. Blood gushed from his bite on my right hand. Cousin Bill wrapped his red handkerchief around my palm and had me hold a steady pressure over the wound as we drove to Dr. Faust's office. My four partners watched while the professional sewed me up. We all agreed ending a rat's life using the humane procedure was too risky. My business associates and I decided that sometimes the old tried and true ways were the best and went back to using the blunt end of a hatchet.

One afternoon my younger brother Larry and I were on our way home from checking traps for our muskrat and mink fur enterprise. I was driving our family car and traveling along around 25 miles an hour. I lacked experience driving on public roads. Larry wanted to help drive and tried to shift the automatic transmission leaver from his seat on the passenger side of the car. I remember asking him to stop, telling him he risked causing an accident, but he was determined. My eyes left the road for a moment as I pushed his hand away a second time, and in one sweeping motion my left hand turned the family car into an aged walnut tree.

The sound of the crash and glass shattering has never left my memory. My twelve-year-old brother was hunched over in the passenger seat. He was not moving. I crawled out of the car with blood dripping from my face, ran around the back and pulled open the passenger door. I wasn't sure Larry was still alive when I pulled him from the car and laid him on the ground. I dashed to Uncle Dean's farmhouse. He called for an ambulance and we both rushed back to the accident scene. By that time Larry had been loaded into the ambulance. Mother was at his side. The ambulance was driving away when the police arrived along with Frank Painter, a neighbor and an accomplished attorney.

Mr. Painter stood beside me as the police asked their questions. I heard the professional litigator say, "Those walnut trees are sure close to the road," and, "It's a little foggy tonight," as though he was already preparing for a trial. The policeman asked me for my driver's license. I gave him my farm permit and explained we had finished running our muskrat traps and were on the way home on the road. I was nervous and more interested in getting to the hospital to see my brother than talking with the police. The two officers and Mr. Painter discussed whether trapping animals qualified as farming and if I should have been on a public road. With a competent attorney standing next to me and both of our concerns for my brother, the police finally agreed that trapping was a form of farming and my permit for driving was acceptable. Uncle Dean and Aunt Helen loaded me into their car and we headed for W. A. Foote Memorial Hospital.

Larry was in surgery when we arrived. Mother said they expected him to survive, but he had serious facial abrasions. The doctor stitched my lip where my teeth had penetrated and sent me to surgery to reattach a severed tendon on my right hand. A quarter-inch steel ball attached to a wire protruded from below the skin on my hand for weeks after the incident. I had remarkable dexterity when it was removed. Larry was in the hospital for observation and recovery for three days. Later he underwent plastic surgery to reduce the size of this facial scar. The fur business closed shortly after the accident on the seasoned wisdom of our father.

Willis Farmland

# CHAPTER 9:

## *Timing Is Everything*

Every business starts with a small idea. I am not an inventor or developer of new business concepts. I am an entrepreneur. I organize and operate other people's businesses and sometimes take on greater than normal financial risks to make them work. I look for opportunities that are already up, have potential and can be improved with my expertise.

I have learned when investing in real estate timing is important. In 1972, I was 31 and looking for opportunities for clients, family, and friends. Bob Emmons, owner of a commercial and residential trash collecting and hauling service, presented me with an opportunity.

Bob was a client of our firm. He had purchased a significant amount of land about 15 miles southwest of Jackson on Farwell Lake, developed a good portion of the property and sold the improved parcels at a profit. He offered to sell me the remaining 100 acres for $100,000. We toured the property. The parcel had 1,400 feet of frontage on the lake. The land was prime for development and had opportunity written all over it. I evaluated his offer for a few months and decided to take a chance. It appeared at the time that we could divide the land and double the value.

I didn't have enough money to make the purchase, so I recruited two more investors: John Parker, MD and James Ekleberry, DDS. They were both clients and Jackson area doctors. We formed a partnership, the Farwell Lake Investors, and each contributed a third of the capital required to buy the land. The partnership called for us to share in the profits or losses equally and that I would do most of the work without additional compensation, which followed my philosophy of doing my share and a little bit more.

Going into this venture, I could see we would need additional capital to complete the development cost, which is one reason I invited the others to partner. More participants mean more investment capital with which to work, ensuring enough money to complete the project and maximize its potential. In the first phase of development we hired a surveyor, Richard Gutekunst, to divide the land. Michigan's development laws permitted four small parcels from the whole with the rest having to be at least 10 acres.

The surveyor came up with a creative layout of the land, maximizing the number of splits. He had four small parcels on the lake and eight ten-acre parcels with a winding road down the center. Gutekunst completed the survey and staked it out with lot numbers. His plans exceeded our expectations and proved it pays to hire a professional.

The economy was going well in Michigan in 1972 and I was optimistic. A third of the property was mine. The other two partners had control. I had confidence in their judgment and integrity. We were all ready to make a ton of money.

An opportunity was presented to the partners during the design process. We had a once-in-a-lifetime opportunity to name a road. Discussions ensued with the partners, family and friends, talks that turned out to be more of a challenge than we anticipated. Naming the street after a famous person or family member did not fit our goal. We agreed the name should match the location and describe our vision of the neighborhood. Leisure Lane became the perfect fit.

We hired another expert, friend, and client. Patricia Stover was an energetic, motivated, and eager real estate salesperson. She spent a significant part of each summer on Farwell Lake at a cottage that had been in her family for decades and seemed like the perfect person to sell the lots. The marketing and promotion started strong, but sales remained alarmingly silent. We did sell one 10-acre parcel to a neighbor for $10,000.

The Middle East oil-producing countries shut the U.S. off from their oil supply shortly after we placed the property on the market. A 25-cent gallon of gas during the oil embargo of 1973-74 shot up to $1.25 a gallon. In today's economy that five-fold markup would be comparable to gas going from $3 to $15 per gallon. The negative factor back then was not only the increase in price. The future price of gas was unknown. The economy took a dive. The greatest impact on the market for real estate at that time was a destination requiring a short commute to work or play.

The cost to maintain the Farwell Lake property was relatively low. We had no debt and property taxes were low. We did manage to sell another lot to a family who built the first home on the property. It was not the quality of home we were hoping for, but the sale did show activity and it gave us working capital for the prosperous future we all anticipated.

The economy nationwide began to improve. We became optimistic. This would surely bring buyers. Then another oil embargo hit in 1979 causing not only inflation but also a sharp increase in interest rates. The prime rate shot up to 20% and lending was stalled. The home development market continued to be flat and the country was in for a long-term recession. I had patient partners who understood the situation. I disclosed our financial situation frequently and honestly. The years moved on. We persevered.

In contrast to the real estate market, my entry into the CPA profession was timed perfectly. The accounting business was growing by leaps and bounds. Audits required in the governmental sector had exploded. We seized each opportunity. The service performed outside our normally busy winter season utilized our staff to its fullest, which, in turn, swelled the bottom line of our firm.

The economy stabilized near the end of the '80s and a couple of Farwell Lake parcels sold at our initial offering price 14 years before. Sales began to return some of our invested capital.

An unfortunate event took place in the late 1980s that still is vivid in my mind. One of our partners, my friend Dr. Ekleberry, developed a terminable disease that took his life. I spent time with his family during his illness, and after his passing continued the relationship with his children who were then in high school. I helped them settle and design their future financial affairs.

The passing of Dr. Ekleberry gave the Farwell Lake Investors a new partner, Mrs. Ekleberry, and a new experience. There was no provision in our agreement for the remaining partners or a life insurance policy to buy out a deceased partner. Pat Ekleberry was now included in all communications of the partnership that had been in existence for 15 years. I learned from this incident to look ahead and make long-term plans in whatever I do.

We entered the '90s still owning most of the property. The partners did feel better about the economy, but sales remained slow. Pat Stover was still with us as the realtor and brought us a relative who purchased a lakefront lot for speculation rather than building a home. The client bought it for our 1974 price of $25,000. Wow, we now had money in the bank.

A neighbor bought another lot from us, giving him 20 acres to build a beautiful home. Property began to move and by 1994 we had sold all the lots at or just above our initial offering price. At this juncture, we were more interested in getting out of the venture than holding on for higher prices. After all, it had been 20 years since we purchased the property from Bob Emmons, who by this time was also deceased.

We sold the last 10-acre parcel for $38,000 to our good friends Dick and Peggy Lowe who lived in the area. We were thrilled to be out of the land-development business and went out to celebrate. We were curious about what our buyer had in mind to do with this land and soon found out. We discovered he was wiser and smarter than we were. He became a mini-developer.

According to Michigan law, every 10 years that passed offered a new opportunity to create four more lots from the original 100 acres of property. Our buyer seized the opportunity and divided the property into four lots. The restrained housing market turned around and was going great guns in 1995. He sold all four lots at an average price of $30,000 per lot, profiting nearly $80,000 within the first year.

Our Farwell Lake Investors profited about $30,000 over the 20 years, which equated to 1% per year on the money. Talk about timing, my friend was on the high end and we were on the low end. Unlike us, he entered the market at the beginning of the tech stock market run-up that produced extraordinary profits. It's hard for me to imagine that the original lake lots we sold for

$28,000 have resold for more than $250,000. Timing is everything.

The cycles in the real estate market are generally driven by entirely unpredictable events. In our case, declines were based on two oil embargoes and high interest rates. Low interest rates started to drive the recovery. Then hot stock markets fueled the value of real estate. Following a short decline in the early 2000s, real estate values were spurred again by easy credit and mortgages.

Bob Emmons had great timing in selling the land to us in 1974 at a good price for him. We sat on the land for 20 years with very little appreciation. Others made substantial money in short periods of time on the resale of their lots. Real estate is usually an excellent investment but can go through cycles that may vary from five to 20 years, depending on location. I love the cliché, "I would rather be lucky than good!" That frequently happens with timing.

Occasionally I take a drive down Leisure Lane and feel great satisfaction in being the leading partner in that development. There are more than 15 homes in the development today, giving many families the opportunity to enjoy the beauty of nature provided by Farwell Lake.

My core business, Phil Willis CPA, was doing well. I focused on the future, on new investments where I could positively influence the results. The new ventures developed more work for the firm, and at the same time provided new relationships and additional opportunities.

I was careful in the new transactions to be adequately capitalized, to retain cash reserves, and to limit the downside risks. Early on, my goal was to start building a portfolio of companies that could operate independently, generate ongoing cash flow, and create value.

# CHAPTER 10:

## *Perseverance*

A lifetime of working on the farmland I would eventually inherit was not for me. My desire to be a dealmaker was in my DNA. My great-grandparents and grandparents were entrepreneurs. While working the farm they looked for business ventures that would improve the quality of their lives and that of their families. So did my dad. He managed the farm he inherited from his parents at 2215 Willis Road, and purchased a second farm on Craft Road. He paid cash for the new land and leveraged the work between the two properties with hired men and their families.

Dad was determined to educate my brother and me in machinery maintenance and safety. He would go over the details of each piece of equipment and remind us how to use it safely again and again. "Turn off the power takeoff and shut off the tractor each time you dismount." Frequently the equipment would clog with crops or soil and require manual clearing of the sharp blades, conveyors, and moving parts. That was the danger in operating farm equipment. We followed Dad's instructions and survived with minimal injuries. Larry and I sustained more injuries playing on the farm and during high school sports than we did working on the land. We kept Grass Lake's Doctor Faust busy for years stitching our wounds closed.

My father was a visionary and saw the farm equipment business as the wave of the future. He partnered with Ford Smith in 1944 and the two men opened a state-of-the-art facility to sell International Harvester farm equipment. They named the building at 142 W. Michigan Avenue in Grass Lake the Grass Lake Implement Company. Who knew this building would be important in my life 74 years later?

Later that business expanded to include sales of General Electric appliances and Spartan televisions. Spartan, based in Jackson, manufactured one of the first televisions in the world and became a popular brand nationwide. Dad was an astute businessman and later added Ford automobiles to the product line. This was rewarding to him because his father sold Ford Model T's around 1910. Dad's business sold such a variety of products it was becoming what we now know of as a smaller version of "Walmart."

My family worked on the farm during summers while growing up, but we relied on hired men to do the vast portion of the labor. Dad and Mom were set on their two sons attending college and becoming car dealers. At the time I probably would have followed their wishes, but to be honest, I would not have been happy selling cars.

My opportunity of a lifetime came when Dad helped me get a summer internship. Neither one of us realized it at the time. The job followed my sophomore year at Albion College, a private liberal arts school near Jackson where I majored in Economics. Dad had influenced my financial and management skills, but I had not zeroed in on the desire to become a CPA. The internship came about because Dad asked his accountant if he had a summer job for me. Getting me that job was the best thing my father ever did for me. What a door opener that turned out to be. I went back to the same company and interned the next summer.

Sadly, Dad passed away of a heart attack when he was only 59. His death was unexpected. We were shocked and grieving, but we still had to deal with it. I was 21.

His share of the business was sold to his partner, Ford Smith. That freed Larry and me of the obligation to follow his footsteps in the car business.

Our mother, Lois Snyder Willis, stepped up to the challenge and became our family leader. She, like my father, was a great mentor in terms of financial responsibility and success. Larry and I assisted Mother in the farming operations. I learned a great many business skills managing a dairy farm. And for us, there was no safety net. The three of us had to make it work.

My graduation from college with a bachelor's degree in business and economics with minors in sociology and psychology landed me a job at the CPA firm of Young, Skutt & Britenwischer as a staff accountant. It was then that I set my sights on becoming a Certified Public Accountant.

I dedicated all my spare time to passing the CPA exam. I understood the three-day event was the toughest professional exam to pass. Prerequisites required the student be an accounting major from an accredited college with two years' experience employed as a public accountant. I enrolled in the University of Michigan part-time while continuing to work at YS&B, studying nights and weekends to earn the equivalent of an accounting major.

The exam consisted of six parts and was offered once every six months. Entrants had to pass at least two parts to get any credit. College was behind me by almost two years at this point. Although a bit anxious, I signed up to take the exam with a high level of confidence. I had to work for my grades in high school and college. I was a good student, but not a great one. By now I was married to Carolyn, my study habits were not as sharp, and the laws had changed in the fast-paced world of public accounting.

Someone told me only 10% of the applicants pass the first time they take the exam. I took the exam and passed Economics, my college major, and failed the remaining five sections. I can tell you it was a humbling experience. The philosophy of the profession and testing board was that only the best, most qualified people enter the CPA profession. They had to represent the highest quality in knowledge, integrity, and ethics.

Six months later I sat for the exam again, this time passing auditing but failing Economics along with the other four parts. All that effort and still I had earned no credits toward my certification. To say I was discouraged would be an understatement. I began to wonder if I really had what it takes to become a CPA. I had dedicated more than two years toward my goal since graduating from college yet had made very little progress. I gained valuable experience and training, of course, which qualified me for internal accounting jobs at small companies, and I had a few interviews and job offers. But I dreamed a bigger dream. I wanted more. I had a larger vision for my life.

I could see that becoming a CPA was a monumental challenge, so I made a 100% commitment, signed up for an extension course, and dedicated two nights a week and Saturday mornings for studies. I have always loved the outdoors and sports, and I can tell you there were many beautiful summer mornings when I looked out the window and daydreamed of doing anything besides studying. But I closed the shades and kept my nose to the grindstone. Somewhere deep inside I knew I could have the life I longed for even if the evidence was not leaning in that direction. I worked 40 to 50 hours a week, and I studied at least 10 additional hours.

Six more months passed as I prepared for the exam. I was back in the now-familiar classroom along with hundreds of others eager to become CPAs. I did not pass the entire exam, but at least I passed two sections, Theory of Accounting and Business Law. Somehow, I failed Auditing and Economics and the rest. Go figure. I had passed Auditing before. I had passed four out of the six sections at one point or another. I continued believing I would accomplish my goal.

The next sitting of the exam was critical because of the rules made by the lords of the American Institute of Certified Public Accountants, AICPA. If I did not pass at least two more parts, I would lose my previously earned credits and would have to start over again. It seemed to me like these rule-makers stayed up nights dreaming of new hurdles. The pressure was on. I was excited to sit once again for the exam. It was confidence mixed with a healthy measure of apprehension. The results arrived. I passed Auditing and Economics. Hurray! It was time for a bit of a celebration.

By this time, I had more than three years' experience and only had to pass the final two sections of the exam, Practical and Auditing. I continued my preparation and felt ready for the next exam. I walked out of the test room after a day and a half convinced that I had written the best Auditing answers ever. I really thought it was perfect. Two months later I learned that I passed Practical and flunked Auditing.

I almost threw in the towel. I was stunned, yes, but my stubborn streak surfaced. I became determined to become a CPA or I would die trying, darn it! The next exam was May 1967, four years after I had begun my career in public accounting. This became personal, like the challenge to do that last crunch when your abs scream, "*No mas.*" I took the test for the sixth time and awaited my results.

Friends and colleagues who had passed the test told me if I passed the exam, the envelope containing my results would be addressed Phil Willis, CPA. It was time for the envelope. I wondered if my hard work and perseverance would pay off this time or be just another humiliating disappointment. A call came for me at the office. It was my wife, Carolyn. "Great news! You passed!"

Every golfer knows that when you hit a hole-in-one, after the 18th hole, you buy the cocktails in the clubhouse. The same tradition was true in our office. All drinks were on the new CPA at a celebration after work. It was my great pleasure to pick up the tab that night. Four years of perseverance had paid off, and soon I would receive my CPA certificate, #4987.

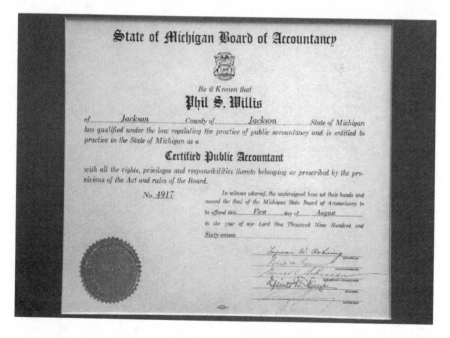

# CHAPTER 11:

*Seizing an Opportunity*

More opportunities and responsibilities were possible for me after passing that exam. My ultimate goal was to own my own firm, but how that would happen was unclear. One day I happened to notice an ad in the *Jackson Citizen Patriot*. It was just a small piece. "CPA Wanted." When faced with an opportunity, if possible, I like to take a brief time-out to think, imagine the situation from different angles, and run it through my gut-meter.

I thought about it for 24 hours before calling for an appointment. Bob Campbell was the son of the CPA who had recently passed away. It turned out that Bob had an opportunity to work with one of his accounting clients in his family firm, Central Advertising. Bob was eager to begin working with the billboard advertising company and did not want to continue working in his father's firm. He offered to sell me 50% of the business, and the remainder after five years, if I was successful.

I reviewed the financials of both companies. The outdoor advertising business was more successful than the CPA firm. I was excited at the possibility of owning an accounting company, but I didn't have my certificate yet. Without that, I was not allowed to own a CPA firm or issue audits.

Then the lords of the AICPA threw more hurdles in my lane. They required five written recommendations from clients I had worked with. And, they needed to complete their report of my legal background, checking for arrests and convictions. There was an additional $100 fee to pay. The last part was easy, and I assumed there would be no trouble with the legal part, except for the time it took to do the research in pre-personal computer days. Getting the written recommendations would take some time and hold everything up. I decided to sleep on it for a couple more days.

I phoned Bob Campbell to meet with him again. I explained my situation. Before I could purchase his company, I needed to receive my certificate. In the meantime, I realized I was taking a risk that someone else would see this opportunity and move on it. I was also aware that clients were leaving the Campbell CPA firm because there was no CPA on site. I did something I rarely do. I procrastinated, that is until a life experience helped me make my decision.

The YS&B firm had a policy regarding taking time off. An employee could take comp time in the summer if he was not busy as an offset against overtime he had worked during the winter. Things were slow at the office in late August, so I set up a Thursday afternoon golf game with some other professionals in the community. Following company policy, I requested the Thursday afternoon off on the previous Tuesday. The lead partner asked me if I had checked with other partners to see if they had work for me. I replied that I had and that they had all said it was fine for me to play golf. The boss said he would look for some work.

I called my boss Thursday morning to get the okay. He said he was still checking and would let me know. I had reserved a tee time of 12:30 p.m. By noon I had still not heard back, so I called the others to let them know I would not be there. At 12:30, I was given permission, but now it was too late.

That incident changed my life. I seized the opportunity, called Bob Campbell and we met that Saturday morning for five hours. Negotiations began for me to buy into the A. J. Campbell CPA firm. I learned from the experience that if employees want time off and have complied with procedures, they should be able to enjoy their leisure time.

Bob and I had a lot of faith and trust in each other. We two accountants drew up the legal documents for our CPA venture to begin September 30, 1967. The final contract was three pages long. In those days, it was common to make a contract or agreement with a handshake, especially in small towns like ours. There were some complexities in the one-of-a-kind agreement. We did need some things in writing since initially it was a five-year agreement with my buying 50% of the firm up front and purchasing the remaining portion in five years. Today it would require two attorneys and result in a document of more than 50 pages to make the deal we made back then.

While negotiating the purchase of this business, Carolyn and I were expecting the delivery of our first child, a son we adopted. Scott came after Labor Day, weeks before I was to take over my half of the company. With my growing family did I have doubts? Some, yes, but I was willing to take the risk. There would be future rewards. I was ready to make this commitment and passionately work to make it successful.

Shortly after Scott arrived, Carolyn surprised me with unexpected news. We were expecting. Even though I had heard of this happening, it never occurred to me it would happen to us. We later teased each other that on Labor Day 1967 we had no children and on Labor Day 1968 we had two sons.

When I gave my two-week notice to my boss, he asked about my plans. We discussed it and he told me flat out that I would not make it. I thought for a moment and replied, "Maybe not, but I am going to give it my all." A couple of days later, he called me into his office saying he had a proposal. He suggested that we buy A.J. Campbell's firm as partners. I thought for a second and said, "No, thanks!"

I did buy the firm, even with a new baby and one on the way. I had no experience running a business. I was 27. All the employees were older than me. I was determined to make a success of it.

The A.J. Campbell firm had three full-time employees with experience in bookkeeping and taxes. There was no CPA on site and the firm was spiraling downward since the death of its founding principal. Bob introduced me to the employees ahead of the date for my participation and we found ourselves to be a good match. I began working on a schedule and he started introducing me to clients, from whom I also received a good reception. I spent my time managing the business and learning as much as I could about our clients. I was looking to understand their needs as well as their desires to grow their companies and to offer them more and improved services. I asked lots of questions of the staff, like who were our former clients and why did they leave?

I was told A.J. Campbell CPA had audited the Jackson Public Schools, the largest school district in Jackson County. No one in my company knew the status of the current audit or if the CPA firm was performing it. I looked at this as a potential opportunity and called their finance director, Byron Love. I went to his office that same day and introduced myself. I asked him about the audit and he replied that he was confused about what was going on at A.J. Campbell, but that if we could start soon, we could have the job. I assured him that we could start the next day, and we did.

We handled all the challenges with research and due diligence and completed our assignment ahead of time including a letter of suggestions and recommendations to improve the operations of the district's finances. Our report was presented, and Mr. Love accepted our recommendations, authorizing us to perform additional services. We were the smallest firm in the county at the time performing an audit for the largest school district in the area. I was proud to get the job. Since fall is the slowest time of the year for a CPA firm, having the work for the Jackson Public Schools was especially beneficial. We were able to add to our bottom-line, which impressed Bob Campbell. He soon allowed me to buy the other half of the company at the end of one year instead of five as we had agreed. I was all for that.

We looked for and found more opportunities. Bob became partners with A. P. Cook III and Max Lorencen in Central Advertising. They were building an extremely successful billboard company across Michigan. Bob's new job was much less confining than managing the CPA firm. He saw the firm as baggage. I saw it as an opportunity. He has complimented me many times on how I managed the business. He said he never had a single complaint from any of the clients I assumed in the acquisition. Bob passed away in 2015. I so appreciated his confidence in me. You've heard the phrase "One man's trash is another man's treasure." I try to keep that in mind when looking for opportunities.

Corporations may elect the month in which their 12-month year will end. They do this for tax-planning advantages or to have it at a slow time of their annual business cycle. We refer to this as a fiscal year end verses the common December year-end. This practice is essential in good CPA firm management, enabling us to meet the clients each quarter and to spread some of our work over different periods throughout the year. A. J. Campbell had set the pace and done a good job of balancing the work year. The main benefit is utilization of your primary asset, the firm's employees. I believe people are the most important asset of any organization. Good employees will take care of our clients. Slowly but surely, we turned the firm around from the downhill slide to an upward growing business.

My first two prize clients were school districts whose leaders I had met at my previous employer, Springport and Grass Lake Schools. We received commitments from both about nine months after I took over at A. J. Campbell. This was especially good because the services they required could be done during the summer months after our busy tax seasons.

Taking a small salary during the year, a nice bonus at year-end and operating with more than adequate cash in the bank made sense to me. I frequently utilize a bank line of credit to provide additional capital if I need opportunity money.

With my family growing we planned to buy a larger home. I timed the purchase to coincide with my year-end bonus. That would provide the down payment. Our firm was beginning to build assets. The most valuable asset we had were our clients who became friends for life. We are still serving several of these same families today, most of whom are now third generation adults who have continued family businesses or started their own. My colleagues and I are all grateful to have had the opportunity to mentor and watch these children grow to become savvy, business-minded adults.

# CHAPTER 12:

## *Dealing with Change*

Sitting there with *TransAction* stuck on the sandbar and with the Intercostal Waterway swirling around us gave me time to think. Usually reasoning a problem all the way through produces a winning solution. We worked out several scenarios and finally concluded we didn't have enough experience to attempt this job. We could not chance damaging the vessel. I have learned to do what I love, like, and am good at and let other people do what I am not qualified or comfortable doing. The painful lesson learned from that muskrat's bite reminded me I am not a professional waterway captain. We needed to ask an expert for help.

I contacted a towboat service on channel 16 of our VHF radio and asked what the charge would be to pull us off. The man on the other end of the radio sputtered, "The minimum would be $800 but it could run more depending on the difficulty of the job."

$800? Shocked, I then recalled the wisdom in the lyrics of Kenny Roger's song. "If you're gonna play the game, boy, you gotta learn to play it right." I should know this game by now. I have been negotiating with and for my clients for 30 years. So, I tried my skill with the towboat service.

The scoundrel would not budge. I thought, you've got to know when to hold 'em, and tried another tactic. I offered the guy cash. He stood firm. $800. This was my introduction to the cost of boating. I would eventually learn everything on a boat costs three to 50 times what it would to maintain a car.

The man at the towboat service shocked me out of my haggle-induced stupor. "Sir! Sir, the tide is going out! What do you want to do?" I realized then that if we did not get pulled off soon, we could be stuck here until morning. Pat would be unhappy missing our dinner date with friends. It was time to "fold em'". Negotiations were over. I asked the opportunist. "How soon can you get here?"

Waiting for the tugboat service seemed like an eternity. I found myself humming know when to run, when I remembered a lesson I learned from what I thought was the investment opportunity of a lifetime, the seven hotels we constructed and purchased over a period of years.

We sold four of them at a loss when it was "time to run". We walked away. Three were extremely successful ... like oil gushers in Texas or cash cows on a farm. We held on those. I have used Kenny Roger's wisdom in business dealings over the years as well as in my family life.

I married my first wife, Carolyn, in the summer of 1962 just after completing my junior year of college. My father had died a month before the wedding.

Carolyn was a good mother and family person. She took good care of our two sons, Phil and Scott. She maintained a great household providing us with wonderful home-cooked meals. But Carolyn and I had our differences. We had grown apart as a couple.

I agreed to go to marriage counseling although I knew I would not change my mind. Carolyn and I met with Dr. Ralph Muhich together and each talked to him privately. On week nine of the ten-week term, Ralph shook his head and said, "Phil, you are holding your emotions inside. You are too consistent. You don't let yourself get carried away. You are too laid back. Someday you are going to go off the deep end and fall out of that canoe into a cold Michigan lake."

My brother questioned my decision to divorce Carolyn. I said, "Larry, I cannot change yesterday. It's history. I can only make the best of the rest of today." I understood what Dr. Muhich was referring to. Sure, I feel stress and hold it in. Every now and then I do yell at someone, but I must be pushed a long way before I react. It's rare that I lose it.

During our last session on the tenth week I told Dr. Muhich. "Ralph, you may tip over in your canoe and freeze to death in a Michigan lake. But I am going to tip out of my canoe in the Caribbean and enjoy the swim."

I was 45 and the boys were 17 and 18 when we divorced. It was the right thing to do for my family.

When Dad died, he left the farm Mother lived on to Larry and me. Larry was 19 and I was 21. My father had prepared his estate plan a few years earlier leaving his spouse other farm property and assets for her to retire on and a parcel of land to my sister, Marilyn. He appeared to be in excellent health at the time and did not anticipate dying anytime soon. My brother and I understood he wanted to keep farmlands in the family to carry on the tradition his ancestors had begun. We were quick to realize the farm, in reality, still belonged to Mother, so we signed a life lease over to her.

My mother, now widowed for 24 years, had become quite comfortable with her independence. She loved to travel, entertain, and play bridge. Mother gave me permission to move back into the farmhouse from where she was wintering in Florida. I transferred two carloads of clothing and personal belongings and shuttled them back into my mother's summer residence. When she returned to the farm in May of 1986, she was pleased to have a companion in her home.

The farm had not changed much since I moved out in 1962. Mother had taken great care of the homestead, but the barns were beginning to show their age. We had discontinued dairy operations 20 years earlier.

As the divorce proceeded, I took solace in my work, comfort in my daily routine with clients and associates, and kept up communications with our sons. Preparing for my future, I told myself this was not a mid-life crisis, but an opportunity. I would not rush into finding a new mate. I would remain single for at least five years and look at the divorce experience and my return to the farm as a new start in life.

Mother and I gave each other space. I was on the go much of the time but enjoyed her company a couple of nights a week. Since my dad's unexpected and premature passing in 1962, any time with my mom was precious. She was an inquisitive woman. She loved to share and discuss ideas. When we had questions, she would research topics at the library or in encyclopedias, and we would discuss what she found. When I considered travel to foreign countries, she researched the best places to go.

Mornings for me began at 5:45 with a workout on a trampoline in the enclosed porch. Mother often came out to talk while I exercised. She did not understand why I would spend time jogging around the property during the rest of the year. People who worked on farms did not need gyms. Daily work was more than enough exercise. Instead, Mom tried to slow me down and have me relax with her. As a project person, I am happiest when moving. Work-related meetings, social and otherwise kept me busy in the evenings. And of course, some dates delayed an early arrival. After all, I was now a bachelor.

Farm before restoration

Mother and I walked the property in July 1986. The summer drought had set in, the grass was brown, and the property looked like a disaster. The place needed maintenance and restoration. My brother Larry, also a CPA in Grand Rapids, kept the farm corporate checkbook. We all agreed the farm buildings had no real economic value and were not generating revenue. We knew returning the farm buildings to what they were originally would not generate cash flow for immediate expenses. The reason for the restoration would have to be to maintain our family's legacy.

The best strategy for owning real estate is to find an investment that generates enough income to cover the expenses of holding the property. The real profit comes in the form of appreciation, or increased value. There are ebbs and flows, but land and real estate generally go up in price and increase in value in the long term. Sophisticated investors refer to the theory as a hedge against inflation. The investment goal is to keep ahead of inflation. Farmland in our area was selling for $100 to $200 per acre in 1962. Fifty years later, in 2016, it sold for $3000 to $5000 an acre.

# CHAPTER 13:

## *Ready for Restoration*

The Willis land holdings near Grass Lake gave Mother, Larry and me a sense of security after Father's death, but now needed attention. It was up to us to maintain what had been entrusted to us. Larry and I understood our generation was the fiduciary for future generations, just as Dad and Mother's was for Larry and me, and his father and mother were before him. This was and still is the Willis family tradition.

Mother and I decided the first restoration project would be the windmill. She had planted a wisteria plant at the base of the structure years ago never envisioning the vine would overtake it. The tendrils clung to the framework, climbing and twining their way up, breaking blades on the windmill, and eventually consuming all the fan blades on top. Having no place else to go, the vine then turned around and grew back down to the ground. Thick leaves covered the windmill. It looked like Jack's Beanstalk.

The woody-stemmed vine, two-inches in diameter, was covered in dense leaves. I could not imagine how the wisteria could be removed without destroying the windmill. Mother had other ideas. She hired a man to cut the vine in sections and then pull parts away with ropes tied to his truck. I thought the whole windmill would tumble. It didn't, and Mother's plan for phase one was a success.

Next, we had to find someone to replace the blades, restore the gears, and paint the top to its original glory. We started our search in 1986 to find someone crazy enough to go to the top of the 35-foot windmill and remove all the broken equipment. I knew from experience it would not be me. We did not have the internet back then, so we started our search by asking friends and neighbors for referrals. We expanded our search to farmers in surrounding counties.

There were not many windmills still standing in Michigan in 1986. There were not many anywhere in the country. My optimistic mother persevered. Our search took us to Indiana in the heart of Amish Country where she tracked down Sam's Windmill Service.

The Amish hold to certain religious and lifestyle beliefs and deeply respect their old traditions. Generally, they use no electricity, no motorized farm equipment, and no cars. They operate with horses, buggies, and the same basic farm equipment used over a hundred years ago.

The Amish came to the farm, dismantled and removed the top section of the windmill and then disappeared. I prayed they would return it one day in working order. My prayers were answered with a phone call two months later. Sam said they would arrive to restore the windmill the following week and fulfill their contract as promised. The Amish workers installed the top section in a condition that was as good as new. The fan blades work as well today as they did nearly 100 years ago. Our Baker Run-in-Oil steel windmill, first introduced to the marketplace in 1923, was back working. And it was beautiful.

Phase one of our project was complete. Mother and I celebrated, she with Cutty Shark and I with Canadian Club on the rocks. We toasted to future generations that would be watching this windmill whirl in the wind on this oasis of precious land. Cheers!

I look at the windmill frequently when I return to the farm these days and remember climbing it when I was about five. At that time, it was used to pump water for the cattle. Larry and I had been looking for something exciting to do one day. I started up the ladder first and Larry, who was only three, followed close behind. When I reached the top, I looked down. "Holy cow!" My body froze stiff as a board and I held on for dear life.

Willis Windmill 1986

I begged Larry to go down and get Mother, which he did. A few minutes later Mother came to the rescue. She called for me to climb down but I could not let go. Literally paralyzed with fear, I pleaded with her to come to the top of the windmill and save me. In her cotton housedress and black leather, two-inch-heeled, laced-up shoes, she climbed the narrow metal steps of the 35-foot windmill. Once at the top, she gently coached me to climb down with her.

Mother has always advised me to find my passion and give it all I've got. I learned that day I was not comfortable with heights. The long-term lesson I learned was to do what I love, like, and good at. If I discover something I am not comfortable doing, I let other people do it. The world needs mountain climbers and scuba divers, hikers who love this land and folks who love and care for animals.

I am not sure why other people develop their fear of heights, but that windmill experience did it for me. I am told that phobias are fears that have no roots. I guess there are things we cannot explain but still must deal with. I was nervous during early airplane flights, and when I looked over the edge of cliffs or anything elevated more than 10 feet. I have learned over the years to face my fears, otherwise I would miss out on living my life.

Lois Snyder Willis, My Mother

# CHAPTER 14:

## *Volunteerism: A Business Training Ground*

The Willis family has lived for generations according to the Bible verse, Luke 6:38. "Give and it shall be given unto you." I remember my father living his life according to the philosophy of doing more than his share for others. As time passed I fine-tuned what has become our family motto into, "Do your share and a little bit more." This philosophy is included in the Willis & Jurasek, CPA's and Consultants' Mission and Value Statements posted on our company website.

My earliest and significant involvement of giving my time to a charitable organization started in 1972 with the March of Dimes, or MOD. We had two young children and knew the importance of healthy children. We believed in the cause. Maureen Beaman, executive director of the local chapter at the time, recruited me to be the MOD Campaign Director. I was hesitant to accept because I was already busy and didn't have a clue what would be involved. Maureen said she would lead me through the process. No problem.

I accepted the position and moved forward with enthusiasm. I was surprised by how many fund-raising events the organization had. I learned recruiters, like Maureen, tell you about the four to twelve board meetings a year, and after you join mention you are expected to be on two committees, each meeting four to twelve times a year. And then there is the homework to prepare for the meetings. I have since learned that if you want to get something done, ask a busy person.

I survived the first year and actually volunteered for another. The challenge for me was to exceed the prior year's fund-raising efforts for each event and surpass the prior year totals. It was rewarding to rise above the goals so Jackson could contribute toward the national goal of helping to reduce birth defects. I was hooked and developed a passion for the MOD.

Three years later they needed someone to step in and chair the local board. Maureen was persistent once again and recruited me for the job. My immediate task was to find a replacement for my old position of Campaign Director.

I had the opportunity to attend the national MOD meeting in Las Vegas in 1973, the first year of my chairmanship. They announced the newest opportunity to raise money was to have a March of Dimes walk. I had never heard of a fundraising walk in our community, or in any other. The National MOD showed results from test markets. They were impressive. They presented a business plan and a new opportunity to raise money.

At our first chapter meeting the idea was presented. The task looked like that of building a small company. We needed to recruit new volunteers. We had to make arrangements with local municipalities and the police department to close streets for the walk. We set up accounting procedures. We developed a marketing and training program for the walkers who in the end raised the money.

We worked the business plan for a year before the first walk. Volunteers were recruited from friends, family, clients, and community professionals. We grew anxious wondering if anyone would show up. And then wondered, would our walkers remember to collect their pledges?

The day arrived. This was the first fund-raising walk to be held in Jackson, Michigan. Our poster child led the walk in a wheelchair. The police department was on hand and the streets were closed. The *Jackson Citizen Patriot* covered the story. Excitement built for all volunteers. Walkers began signing in with their pledges at nine in the morning. We had approximately 300 walkers and raised $5000, a smashing success. Volunteers celebrated with a party that evening where we all began planning next year's event.

We believed in the cause. We had honed our business skills while being volunteers. We gave back to our community and our nation. We met new people. We learned we could recruit and motivate people without giving them money. We gave our time and energy and were rewarded with the self-satisfaction that we had assisted others.

The experience of providing leadership for non-profits goes much deeper for me. Serving as a fundraising leader gave me a chance to explore all areas of management and running a business. Volunteering as a leader in a charity provides an opportunity to gain experience without the risk of loss, plus, a volunteer can determine his or her strengths and weaknesses.

Volunteerism and its requirement for leadership is a lesson in managing or owning a business. Yes, volunteering is an investment in time and maybe even donated money, but a volunteer doesn't have to build an office, buy equipment, or hire staff, which requires a significant amount of cash and usually a personally guaranteed loan from a bank. I am the one at risk in my own ventures. Because of volunteering, people often decide they would rather work for someone else and not have to make tough decisions and risk loss of money or sleep.

I received a phone call one day from Irene Knoak. She and her husband, Lee, had purchased a business and needed a CPA. She reminded me we had become friends while volunteering for the March of Dimes 17 years earlier. The Knoaks were valuable clients until they sold their business and retired.

Subsequently, Irene recruited our CPA firm through our principal Brian Jurasek to do some volunteer tax work for The Jackson Chorale, a local non-profit music group. The cycle of giving and receiving has continued. I never know whom I will meet while volunteering my time and talents or where that relationship will lead, as it did with the Jackson Symphony Orchestra.

Music to my ears as a child was the sound of cattle mooing in the barnyard and roosters crowing from their coop. As I grew older my music became the smack of football pads and crack of a baseball off the bat. Later as I matured into my business career, my music became the ca-ching of the cash register. So, when I was approached by the JSO to join their board, I agreed, but not because I am a music lover. I volunteered because I could contribute my business expertise to a non-profit that was and is the leader in the art and culture of our community. I started as the treasurer and was elected board chairman a few years later. My role as chair provided me with opportunities for introductions to leading musicians and composers, and for speaking engagements. Pat and I have continued to attend concerts and support the JSO at fundraisers long after my term ended.

As I look back over my adult life, I see a pattern in volunteering with charitable organizations. I find it takes two or three years to understand the workings of an organization, its employees and its volunteers. Then it takes another year to be creative and guide the entity toward exceeding their goals. Leadership volunteers only begin to create and benefit the entity in the fourth or fifth year. I think boards that turn over directors every three years are missing the boat in developing their future leaders. And it's the same with building a company. You need people working for and with you who develop a passion for what you're doing and are willing to keep at it.

When I develop enthusiasm for a charity my challenge is to make it more effective than it has ever been. I commit from five to 15 years of my time and energy.

For example, what started nearly 15 years ago as a yearly cookout for Willis & Jurasek employees, clients, friends, and neighbors has turned into a community wide event. We decided to make a fundraiser out of Uncle Phil's BBQ 10 years ago. The event to benefit Jackson area youth has grown in attendance with each year. The 2018 cookout sponsored by some 40 Jackson businesses and associations, hosted nearly 300 guests and earned area youth more than $16,000. Over the years more than $150,000 has been raised to support Jackson area young people as well as other charities.

Me on Longhorn at Uncle Phil's BBQ

My desire to help our young people got a great start and recently benefited Junior Achievement, an organization that works to inspire young people to dream big and reach their potential. We also funded Jackson School of the Arts, an independent school with a mission to make arts accessible to Jackson County youth regardless of their financial means. We have also funded the Lily Missionary Baptist Church after school program. We donated to the Dave Thomas Foundation for Adoption, a voice for foster care adoption with a goal of every child finding a home.

In the early days, I did all the cooking on four round charcoal grills. Now Knight's Steakhouse employees grill chicken and kielbasa on a fire pit 40-foot-long. I got smart after feeling like fried chicken myself at the end of one year's event. That's when I decided to ask others to join Willis & Jurasek in sponsoring the day. Wendy's and Knight's became the other two major sponsors. Each year, charities around the Jackson area are rotated for funding from the BBQ. Some of the other groups that benefit are American Red Cross, Alzheimer's Association, and American Cancer Society.

> "One of the most beautiful compensations of life is that no man can sincerely try to help another without helping himself." Ralph Waldo Emerson

# CHAPTER 15:

## *Growth Through Acquisitions*

As our CPA firm continued to grow with new clients, we needed to hire another experienced accountant. We were looking for a person coming from a similar work culture, one who shared my values, a professional who enjoyed working on a team and understood the demands of the profession. We were looking for an accountant who appreciated family life and raising children in a smaller community. Our aim was to hire someone to carry out the higher-level tasks of a CPA, allowing me more time to focus on client development and management. The best source for good prospects that had the same training, experience and goals was with my former firm.

I had maintained contact with a few of my previous associates and knew some were discontented. I asked Wayne Watters to join our firm. He had grown up in the small town of Morenci, Michigan, which was like Grass Lake. He was active in sports and outdoor activities. He loved his career and wanted to explore new opportunities. It didn't take him long to accept my offer.

I imagine by this time my former boss at YS&B realized he had underestimated me and that I was going to succeed after all.

The urban population of Jackson in 1969 was about 40,000. The county had approximately 150,000. Jackson was a big city to Wayne and me.

Our new office building at 402 Brown Street gave us room to grow. We now had a staff of seven with a considerable amount of experience. Positioned to focus on building the client base and managing the firm, I was not personally locked into servicing a long list of clients. My role was to provide management and a high level of service across the board with all our clients. We worked together as a team.

I spent a substantial amount of face-time with our clients, attorneys and bankers discussing new ideas, and inquiring about the level of our services to ensure we were meeting their expectations. I personally managed some clients with our staff performing the work. Two or more qualified and experienced members of the firm were assigned to each client to develop and build a relationship and service their account.

As we pursued the development of building relationships with clients, attorneys, and bankers, another opportunity arose out of the blue. A sole practitioner CPA died of a heart attack. His name was Donald Gutekunst, the brother of Richard Gutekunst, the surveyor of the Farwell Lake development.

Donald had two employees who did accounting and clerical work. He was the only CPA in the firm. I first heard of his death from a friend, Bill Lee, whose family business used the Gutekunst firm. Bill approached me and inquired about using our firm. Within a day attorney Donald Corley called me, advising me of the passing of Gutekunst, and assessing my interest in purchasing the practice. I jumped at the opportunity.

We met the next day to negotiate a deal with the son of Mr. Gutekunst. Since I had purchased the Campbell firm, I had knowledge of the going rate. We negotiated the deal on similar terms with the exception that the Gutekunst family wanted a two-year payout. We signed the deal the next day, one day before the funeral.

I anticipated the purchase would require more staffing than we currently had and wanted to ensure we could deliver excellent service. The transition of purchasing the firm would take a huge commitment. We needed to contact each of their clients in face-to-face meetings to be sure they would continue with us as their successor CPA firm, and we needed more help. I called Jim Drake, a former work associate. Jim had left the CPA firm and was working as a controller/CFO of a commercial airlines freight company.

Jim accepted my call and responded with enthusiasm. We met and within 24 hours had discussed the opportunity to purchase the Gutekunst firm as partners. We changed the name of our firm to Willis & Drake CPA's. This goes to show how small businesses can pivot quarterly and take advantage of a huge opportunity. We formed the partnership and bought the firm in a period of one week. Jim quickly phased out of his job at the airlines business and hit the CPA business running.

Prior to my partnership with Jim Drake, he worked with his brother Marv who had a bookkeeping/accounting firm. Jim worked out of his home, serving clients in Jackson. Marv worked from his office in Plainwell, a small town north of Kalamazoo. They operated under the name of James Drake CPA. Our merger with Drake added four people and the Gutekunst acquisition added two. We were suddenly a two-office firm with 14 employees. It was a good thing we had Ina Rombyer handling the office. She kept things running like a charm.

Willis & Drake CPA's had an open house at our new office on Brown Street for clients, referral sources, and family. I remember speaking with a special guest, attorney Frank Painter. He was the Grass Lake neighbor who stood by my side when police were questioning me after the car accident. It was 15 years later, and I was 30, now heading one of the largest accounting firms in the city.

Frank congratulated me and asked how the company had come together so quickly. I told him my team had taken advantage of opportunities, that the timing was right, and that certain trends and events were in our favor. I told him I was lucky my Dad got me a job in a CPA firm when the profession was growing. I said I regretted my dad was not here tonight.

Frank Painter, a well-respected attorney in Jackson, was in one of the top two law firms in the area. I was honored to have him attend our first open house. It added to the credibility and respect of our growing young firm. It was also great to have a family friend here. I grew up with his two daughters, Helen Painter Greene and Ruth Painter Kohout. They are both still close to our family today. I refer to them as my "kissing cousins." We could call each other "second cousins" but I prefer the other.

I handled Frank's complimentary comments awkwardly that evening by trying to remain modest and self-deprecating and give credit to others. I have learned since then it is courteous and appropriate to look a person in the eye and say, "Thank you." Now, whenever I am complimented, after my "Thank you," I redirect and give other people the credit.

It might sound disrespectful to be negotiating a purchase of the Gutekunst firm while the owner's funeral was being planned, but I knew clients would find another accounting firm to work with quickly. Two Gutekunst clients had already contacted me. Prospective buyers of the accounting firm may have declined the opportunity because of the risk of client flight with new management or they may have been reluctant because of the cash commitment it would take. Guteunst's attorney, Donald Corley, gave the family some excellent advice. He told them the estate's representative needed to make a quick deal before the clients left and they had nothing to sell.

When Willis & Drake CPA's purchased the new firm, I was 30 and working in the upper level of young professionals in the area. I knew if opportunity knocked, I had to answer the door and do it fast. We had made this acquisition quickly, but we made it with calculated judgment, weighing the costs, revenues, and staffing needed. I applied the same lessons learned while hunting with my father. We had studied the environment, planned and prepared before we pulled the trigger, and we had done it rapidly. We were confident with an additional commitment from our team and two new employees we could continue to meet and exceed clients' expectations.

The acquisition was made with bonus money accumulated over the past year from the firm, my opportunity money. I had been paying my personal bills with positive cash flow and limiting my salary/withdrawals to build cash for future opportunities and investments. I increased my personal cash flow gradually to improve my family's standard of living that was now far better than we ever dreamed it could be.

As I look back on the purchase of both CPA firms, I examine the reasons for the overall positive response we received. We took a personal interest in our clients and placed our efforts and concern for the improvement of each client's business high on our list of priorities.

Owners prematurely taking out too much in wages and benefits and leaving no money in the company for buying power and future opportunities caused the demise of many ventures. Conservatism is a must in building a successful organization. By exercising patience, perseverance, and sacrifice in the early years, future financial rewards should follow as the company grows.

The acquisition of the Gutekunst firm in 1971 opened the door to a multitude of lifestyle opportunities. The one I take pride in the most is meeting new clients and entrepreneurs with similar goals and backgrounds. Our firm still serves many of these family businesses, some of which are in the hands of the third generation and considerably larger than they were back then. We assisted them in navigating the course of growth and evolution to survive and thrive in today's complicated business world. We are proud of their ongoing success. The acquisition also gave us the chance to meet new people that have become our business, social, and lifetime friends. Successful entrepreneurs live their businesses and thrive on the relationships and the friends that become part of their daily lives.

My brother Larry also took the CPA career path. He graduated from Albion College, married his college sweetheart, and moved to Ann Arbor for graduate school at the University of Michigan. He finished his master's degree at the height of the Viet Nam War and was deferred from military service to run the family farm. Larry had substantial responsibilities as farm manager and hired good help. The farm continued to survive under this gentleman farmer's leadership and his golf score handicap was at the lowest level of his life!

# CHAPTER 16:

## *Hunting Adventures*

The Willis family has always harvested wildlife to eat from our farm. We all enjoyed dining on wild game as well as shooting or catching it. Besides rearing Larry and me, my parents raised dairy cattle and poultry. It was a rare occasion that the meat on our dining room table was not from the Willis property.

As a grown man during the mid-1970s, I began going on hunting trips instead of the golfing, skiing, or shopping getaways others enjoyed. I prefer hunting because I love the outdoors, the uniqueness of each trip, and the challenge of catching wild game. I prefer sports requiring active participation to spectator sporting events. I like a five-to-eight-day getaway when I have a chance to clear my mind and focus on the global picture of my life and business. Time in the field is refreshing for me and gives me plenty of opportunity to dream bigger and better.

The days on these hunting trips follow a familiar format. We rise early, lay our plans, and have a big breakfast. We are in the field before sunrise where we hunt for four or five hours and then meet at a central point for lunch. We continue hunting during the afternoon until sunset. Then we meet for beverages where we laugh, tell stories and share highlights of the day. Stories generally revolve around two themes: catching the big one, an animal that grows larger each year in our yarns, and the tales about the ones that got away. We clean up, sometimes take a nap, and head out for dinner – also a time filled with more good stories and great food. The differences on these trips center on the game we hunt and the location.

My first trip with the guys was in about 1975 when we took an expedition to Rolfe, Iowa. Organized by Don Hall of Jackson and Lee Kaiser from Lansing, the destination was a small town where Lee's father, a Standard Oil distributor, provided fuel products to most of the farmers in the area. His relationship with the farmers and the Kaiser family had grown over the years. It was easy for Lee, with a strong outgoing personality, to ask permission of farmers to hunt their property. Their land had some of the best soil in the world where corn grew tall and provided food for wildlife year around.

Attorney Charles Nelson and Edward Greene, DVM, both friends from Jackson, joined the hunting party. The five of us drove a motorhome straight through for 22 hours to Fort Dodge, Iowa where we stopped for some breakfast and to buy our hunting licenses. We met later in the day in Rolfe with Lee's family, old friends, and other local hunters.

The common gathering spot for the trip was a local farm where the farmer decorated his property with

Budweiser memorabilia. The second year we hunted in Rolfe we contributed to the decor with the gift of a large Budweiser sign. The farm was a beautiful place with the barns painted white. They called the large barn "the Bud Barn." The lower level contained a huge collection of John Deere farm equipment and an open area for the guests. The upper lofts contained a large assortment of saddles and other horse gear. The atmosphere was complete with live Dalmatians wandering the barns. One end of the loft featured a game room with a small kitchen, card tables, and pool table.

The local restaurant was all set for us at five the next morning. A large buffet and hardy laughter filled the room. Lee went around the tables mapping the farms and sharing strategies for hunters who would hunt in groups of six or seven. He arranged for a dog or two for each group.

We charged out of the restaurant to make it to the fields in time to begin the hunt 30 minutes before sunrise. The temperatures would be in the 40s on most of those early November mornings. The dogs ran in circles obeying their owners' shouts and whistles as they waited for the hunters to take to the fields and marshes. We spread out and headed through the terrain.

The dogs wove back and forth about 20-40 feet in front of the sportsmen. They stopped on "point" when they saw a bird, a signal to the hunters to come forward for a shot. The birds had to be carefully identified because a license permitted shooting roosters only. So, when a pheasant took flight, the closest hunter would holler "hen" or "rooster," and the shooting would begin. Successful shooters would hold up their birds for all to see before tucking them into a special opening in the back of their hunting jackets.

The pheasants were fast, sneaky, and smart. Sportsmen never knew where they would emerge. They generally competed in a running game before they flew, and sometimes sat tight and surprised us from behind. This game bird was more successful at escape than we hunters were at bagging them. I estimate it took three or four shots to bag one bird. The day ended with each hunter generally limiting out with two birds, after which we would all head to a local bar for cold beer and stories of the day.

The Rolfe hunting adventure continued for many years. Some years, the Michigan group had as many as 15. I was honored to attend the 25th year, which was highlighted by a plaque from the Iowa governor's office to the Michigan group for our contribution to conservation and to the Iowa economy. By the time I'd made about 18 trips, enjoying each and every one, it was time for me to move on to new territories. I understand the group traveled to Rolfe almost 30 years before it ran its course.

My next hunting trip was to Wyoming for elk in the late 1970s. This trip included Ed Greene, Don Hall, and Robert McCowen, a CPA. We rented a motorhome and pulled a trailer to carry our gear. We returned home with three sets of elk antlers, a few hundred pounds of elk meat, and many cases of Coors beer.

Hunting at the Willis farm has evolved over the last 150 years. Pheasants are rare and duck hunting has lost its popularity. The lure is now white-tailed deer. We have expanded the acreage and have some of the best deer hunting property in the country. Preparation for the local fall hunt is lengthy because I believe in improving and maintaining our habitat for the benefit of the environment, the wildlife, and our neighbors. Hunters are some of the best conservationists in the world. I spend time and money annually working with farmers renting Willis fields to select crop plantings that provide food and cover for the wild game.

Comfort for the sportsmen was not forgotten. We built eight four-by-four condos for hunters elevated on six-foot pilings, and added tree stands across the property to provide observation points. Floors in the condos are carpeted to eliminate noise. Windows on all sides open from the inside. A swivel chair sets in the center. Condo interiors include hooks for excess clothing, binoculars, range finders, and deer-calling devices. And, of course, we have a shelf to place our coffee cup, soda, or water.

We preach and practice gun safety. We limit participation of young hunters to those who have passed hunter safety classes. We follow the laws and deer management practices to ensure an excellent crop of prime bucks every year. When hunters on the Willis farm follow our hunting guidelines they can look forward to taking a larger buck than they ever have before.

The rewards from the enjoyment of deer hunting have led to the reconstruction of an old dairy barn at 2215 Willis Road. We dismantled the barn originally built in the 1860s, and retained the timbers, wooden pegs, and support beams. We poured a new concrete foundation and floor to support the structure and have restored the original timbers and beams to their old glory. The barn is not used for cattle anymore, although from the outside it looks as if they would be welcome. The building is now a man-cave and welcoming center for hunters, friends, and relatives.

Me and his Honor Chuck Nelson

# CHAPTER 17:

## I Bought Out The Wrong Partner

A computer service owner approached me in 1970 looking for an investor to buy out his partner. My vision was that computers would soon dominate the financial industry, so I listened. I didn't know it at the time, but I was about to learn that even a business acquisition planned by an experienced CPA could run amuck, and that it could become a valuable and costly lesson.

I visited the Specialized Computer Service's clean, climate-controlled environment. The computer filled the entire building. Cards punched with accounting data were entered into a machine that sorted the data and printed out various reports. The cards could be reentered to print data into different reporting formats. SCS had eight customers renting or sharing the company's services primarily in the payroll check-writing arena. I recall their largest customer was W. A. Foote Hospital. Impressed, I began my due diligence.

The four employees included the owners. Mr. Talker was the sales person. He was the owner who approached me to buy out his partner, Mr. Joe, the company's computer whiz. Two additional employees operated the systems, and I was led to believe they could do the programming as well.

I analyzed financial statements and could see cash flow was adequate to cover operating expenses and service the debt. SCS had been purchasing their building on a land contract. Their computer manufactured by NCR used Cobalt programming software that was so complex that few techies understood or knew how to program back then. Those who did were the geeks of that era.

I spoke with Mr. Joe and felt comfortable with the acquisition of 50% of the business. Our CPA business cash flow was good. I had my savings reserve; my opportunity fund I could use for financing. I moved forward with the buyout and entered the computer service industry.

We transferred the bookkeeping and accounting to our CPA firm where I could keep a close eye on the finances and cash flow. SCS operated well for the first few months, but growth was flat. Mr. Talker and I met regularly to prospect for new customers, but the long list of contacts produced no new clients. He was unable to close a sale.

It the meantime I keep my focus on my bread and butter business that consistently produced cash flow and generated opportunities to expand or invest in other areas, my CPA firm.

It did not take long for me to realize I had bought out the wrong partner. Mr. Talker did not understand the programing or benefits of the service he was selling. He could not convince prospects that the service added value to their companies or that it would save them money. It turned out that Mr. Talker had been getting the leads and Mr. Joe, the former techie, had been closing the sales.

Problems at SCS began when we missed our client's service deadlines. We began to lose customers. Then we experienced negative cash flow. In order to make the payments and payroll, I made deposits in SCS from my personal savings. I decided to exit the business after a year and I told my partner, Mr. Talker, to find me a buyer. He had found me, so I figured he could find another investor.

A few more months went by. The words *I bought out the wrong partner!* kept running through my mind as I continued pouring money into SCS. Closing the business was not an option. It would have resulted in a huge personal loss to me. I would have had to continue paying for the computer and the building with no income. Mr. Talker continued to look for a buyer. I remained calm and patient and kept telling myself not to panic and yell and scream. I was sure SCS had potential for someone, but not for our current combination of owners and management.

Mr. Talker showed up at the office one day with a prospective buyer for my share of the business. I listened to their proposal and decided to pursue the opportunity. I was anxious to cut my losses. The new buyer would take over SCS as is but did not want the building. The sale price was zero.

I knew a little about real estate and decided to accept the offer. The benefit of the sale was that it stopped the "bleeding" of cash flow. The challenge now was to sell the empty building.

I placed it for sale and soon had a buyer. This business opportunity had cost more than my Albion College education. I was happy to see SCS continue for many years - from a distance. It was a valuable learning experience for me. I think of it as the SCS silver lining.

# CHAPTER 18:

## Doors Continue to Open

Our firm continued to expand over the next few years, nothing as sensational as the purchase of other firms, but a nice steady controlled growth. It was the kind of expansion that permitted us to develop employees in line with the client load, so we could maintain trained and experienced staff to serve our valued clients.

One of the early additions to the firm, Wayne Watters, finally passed the CPA exam, a challenge that took me six tries to complete. Wayne worked with us for another year before Jim Drake and I decided to honor him and change the name of the firm to Willis, Drake & Watters CPA's. We believed it would give our firm more depth in our marketing potential for larger clients.

The 1970's were turbulent years for the nation's economy. The Economic Development Corporation, EDC, of Jackson County was formed to provide tax-exempt bonds for eligible businesses. I was invited to be one of the founding directors in 1977 and served as the treasurer of the initial board.

Today the bonds, called Industrial Revenue Bonds, or IRB's, offer a substantially lower interest rate in the public market because the interest paid on the bonds is tax-free. Securing the bonds is complex and expensive. The procedure includes hiring an independent trustee, a re-marketing agent, and a bond-rating agency like Standard and Poor's, Inc. The business applying for the bonds needs to get a Letter of Credit, LOC, from a large bank, and must have an excellent credit rating. The stronger the bank's credit rating on Wall Street, the lower the interest rate would be on the bonds. Those industries qualifying in the initial years were broad and included almost all businesses investing in real estate or industrial equipment.

The IRB's became immediately popular because interest rates in the country were out of sight. Imagine, the prime rate was 20%, making it nearly impossible to piece together a financing package. A 15-year project could cost three times the value of the project. Inflation paralleled the interest rates, or I should say, interest followed the inflation.

Inflation was brought about by several factors, but it primarily followed the price of oil. During the 1973 Arab-Israeli War, Arab members of the Organization of Petroleum Exporting Countries, OPEC, imposed an embargo against the United States in retaliation for the U.S. decision to re-supply the Israeli military and to gain leverage in the post-war peace negotiations. The price of oil increased in multiples of five or six times within a year. This happened twice during the '70s with the latest in 1977.

I enjoyed being involved on the EDC board of directors. I was learning about the broader-based financial world and had a first-hand look at the companies in Jackson County that were expanding, which yes, provided more prospects for the CPA business.

With continued growth came the need for more office space. We called a local architect to discuss an addition on our 402 South Brown Street office. He recommended it would cost less to add on to the facility than it would be to build a new office. He drew up plans and placed them out for bid. The bids came in more than double the estimates! We decided to scrap the addition project and build our own office. The search for a new site began.

We looked at various locations around town. Most folks in our organization lived or grew up in the wide-open spaces of the country. The idea of a building site on land with room where employees and clients could park near the entrance appealed to all of us. We found a beautiful wooded site on the outskirts of Jackson on Spring Arbor Road.

Millard Ordway, the owner, had been developing a residential subdivision on the back part of his 75-acre parcel and was reserving the road frontage for office development. I did some research and determined Mr. Ordway needed money to complete the infrastructure for the residential portion of the development. But, he was not ready to sell.

I called Mr. Ordway every month asking him to sell us the road portion of the property. The answer was "no" each time, that is, until a year had passed. He was finally ready to talk. Negotiations did not take long. He was now eager to move forward.

I wanted to share this opportunity with the principals in our firm because by including them it would help build confidence in the company and add value. We purchased 5.5 acres for $125,000 in 1978. It was the entire frontage on Spring Arbor Road. Our CPA firm chose the prime portion of the land and prepared to build.

Long-term interest rates were 15% in late 1977. It would not have been feasible to borrow at those rates. That's when we turned to the EDC and applied for tax-exempt bonds. We were the second entity to be issued bonds in Jackson County. I loved being on the leading edge of the financial world. The bonds would re-market every week, taking advantage of short-term, tax-exempt interest rates. The rate was about 7.5%, one-half of the going rate for conventional mortgages. Funding was completed, and the project proceeded in earnest. Overseeing construction of our new office and managing the CPA firm kept us so busy we had still not placed the Brown Street property on the market by spring 1978.

The phone rang one day. On the other end of the line was Larry Bullen, a principal in the law firm of Rosenberg, Painter, Stanton and Bullen. My friend and neighbor Frank Painter had passed away and Rosenberg had retired. Larry asked if we would be interested in selling our Brown Street building. I was reminded that timing is everything and said "certainly." I asked who the prospective buyer was. I nearly fell out of my chair when he said it was their law firm.

Rosenberg, Painter, Stanton and Bullen were in a relatively new building in an ideal location near the courthouse. He said they were having difficulty negotiating a lease on the office property owned by Rosenberg. They were looking for an alternative office and wanted to make the decision within 30 days. I was reminded that it pays to know a lot of people.

The law firm purchased our building at our asking price 90 days before we moved to our new offices in September 1978. As it turned out, Bob Campbell and I doubled our money on the Brown Street property. We were trying to do our best every day to maximize our bottom line, and it was working. We had been focusing on the development of new revenue sources, maximizing the return on existing clients, and spending our money wisely. No year had passed that we spent more than we earned, unless it was for a long-term investment. As we made our turnkey transition from the Brown Street property to the Spring Arbor building, I was reminded that sometimes it's better to be lucky than good.

# Economic Development board elects Phil Willis as chairman

By Pat Koschik
Staff Writer

The Jackson County Economic Development Corp. (ECD) today elected as its new chairman Phil S. Willis III, president of the certified public accounting firm Willis and Willis.

Willis was unanimously elected to fill the chairmanship previously held by John H. Schomer, who resigned from the board after a controversy stemming from racial comments he allegedly made at a high school basketball game.

Willis has been the EDC board's treasurer since its inception in 1977.

As the board chairman, he said, his goal is to encourage more small businesses to locate and ex-pand in Jackson County. "Nationwide, they've provided more jobs than big businesses," he said.

Willis said he would promote the use of loan money available from revolving loan funds sponsored by the city and county. John O'Neill, EDC executive director, told board members that the two revolving loan funds have a combined balance of about $400,000, which is waiting for qualified applicants.

Tax exempt bond funding for manufacturers is also available through the EDC, O'Neill said.

Said Willis, "A lot of people give up the idea of starting a business because they figure they can't capitalize it." Money from the re-volving loan fund is available at less than commercial loan rates to people whose business plans in-clude increasing or retaining jobs.

Willis said he also hopes to be-gin a venture capital fund, to be funded by local investors and to provide loan money to qualified people starting new businesses.

Board member Bernard H. Levy, president of Industrial Steel Treating Co., was elected to rep-resent the EDC on the board of the Jackson Alliance for Business Development. Schomer had also served on that board and was its president.

Levy was appointed to the EDC in March to replace Donald Clark, who resigned from the

PHIL S. WILLIS III

EDC board when he retired in January as vice president of oper-ations for the Kent-Moore Tool Group.

---

Copy from the 1977 *Jackson Citizen Patriot* reads:

The Jackson County Economic Development Corp. (EDC) today inducted as its new chairman Phil S. Willis III, president of the certified public accounting firm Willis and Willis.

Willis was unanimously elected to fill the chairman previously held by John H. Schomer, who resigned from the board after a controversy stemming from racial comments he allegedly made at a high school basketball game.

Willis has been the EDC board's treasurer since its inception in 1977. As the board chairman, he said A goal is to encourage more small businesses to locate and expand in Jackson County. "Nationwide, they've provided more jobs then big businesses" he said.

Willis said he would promote the use of loan money available from revolving loan funds sponsored by the city and county. John O'Neill, EDC executive director, told board members that the two revolving loan funds have a combined balance of about $400,000, which is waiting for qualified applicants.

Tax exempt bond funding for manufacturers is also available through the EDC O'Neill said.

Said Willis, "A lot of people give up the idea of starting a business because they figure they can't capitalize on it." Money from the revolving loan fund is available at less than commercial loan rates to people whose business plans include increasing or retaining jobs.

Willis said he also hopes to begin a venture capital fund, to be funded by local investors and to provide loan money to qualified people starting new businesses.

Board member Bernard H. Levy, president of Industrial Steel Treating Co., was elected to represent the EDC on the board of the Jackson Alliance for Business Development. Schomer had also served and was its president.

Levy was appointed to the EDC in March to replace Donald Clark, who resigned from the EDC board when he retired in January as vice-president of operations for the Kent-Moore Tool Group.

# CHAPTER 19:

## *Building Wealth*

My net worth was increasing at a fast pace in 1978. I had been thinking along the lines of building long-term wealth years earlier when a few associates, friends and I formed an investment club. We each researched stocks and presented our findings at our next meeting. The Dow Jones Industrial stock index was near 600 in 1966 when the club started. Fifteen years later, it was still near 600. Growth in the stock market began in 1982. We learned that stock values grow in the long run, that investors must be patient, and that the stock market is not a quick way to make money. We were not lucky investors, but we did learn about good investing.

In 1974, the Employee Retirement Income Security Act, or ERISA, changed the tax code to allow for tax-deductible contributions to an Individual Retirement Account, or IRA. That legislation limited the investment to $1,500 per individual per year. I did not have a lot of cash lying around and lived frugally. I saved and invested first, and then spent what was left. I jumped on this tax-free compounding investment opportunity and today my retirement account has accumulated to six-digit numbers. Unlike my other retirement vehicles this investment is not subject to capital gains or income taxes until you withdraw the money.

Retirement plans offered by employers are good long-term investment strategies because companies match a percentage of employee contributions. An even more significant benefit from retirement accounts is the protection given from litigation under Michigan and other state statutes. The owner of an IRA cannot be forced to cash in a retirement account to pay off debts to creditors in bankruptcy and lawsuit judgments. Spouses, however, are usually entitled to half of an IRA in a divorce.

We shared the opportunity to invest for the future and profit in the appreciation of the property on Spring Arbor Road with our associates. We sold off the excess land on Spring Arbor Road in two sales, one to a group of physicians and the final piece to a dentist. They built beautiful professional offices around us, enhancing the value of our property. We cashed out of the land development partnership with everyone profiting. The greatest benefit was that we basically owned our prime office property for free.

Our CPA firm was operating statewide with three offices in Michigan during the 1970s. Our daily focus was to make every phase of our business better and enhance our client service. We were on the right track and landed some major clients. With growth came circumstances that required major decisions. It was time to grow our audit department and create more specialization.

A niche market opened for our services when a new law required Michigan counties to be audited. Our staff solicited 30-plus counties by mail and phone, engaged in our due diligence and then submitted our proposals. We called the counties the day following the bid opening and got the names and amounts of all the competing firms. Our team monitored the award process, so we would know the competitors' strengths and weaknesses. This gave us the inside track on acquiring new customers and clients. We were successful in getting the contracts for several counties across the state.

Before we sent our well-prepared professional team of auditors to spend a week at the county-client location, our trained staff had phone discussions with the client's accounting staff. Managers and principals planned the risk evaluation based on the entity's financial statements. When the team arrived, they focused their time and effort on the high dollar areas and those with significant risk.

The county audit work was lucrative for us in the '70s because it filled the off-tax-season schedule pipeline. I am a huge believer in the principal that busy people are happy people and that idle staff hours amount to money squandered. Staying busy kept our staff motivated and energized.

The lucrative aspects of this niche business evolved. Uniform standards were set for the work and reports. The buyer who awarded the bids generally did not care who provided the service as long as the price kept going down. It would be like buying corn, wheat, or soybeans on the commodities markets. County audits and those for Michigan's governmental units became a commodity with bids awarded based on price, not service, resulting in minimal profit for us. This is still the case in governmental audits today. We realized our organization needed to reinvent our strengths and focus on more profitable businesses, and I needed to keep my focus on the big picture, not the day-to-day details of the operation.

The partners encouraged participation in our State association, the Michigan Association of Certified Public Accountants, MACPA. We belonged to the American Institute of CPA's and were required to meet continuing education requirements to qualify for membership. These classes provided a broader vision for those working in the daily grind. I liked trying new ideas, changing procedures to keep employees on their toes, keep them alert and thinking. Staff continued their educations and improved their skills. Management offered some the opportunity to join the firm as junior partners or to purchase stock in the company as a carrot for them to stay with the firm long-term and keep involved in management and strategic planning.

I served on the MACPA's Communications Committee, a group that focused on promoting the association's profession to the media and business community. I joined the Annual Meeting Committee that planned the state association's annual three or four-day meeting. Working on this committee turned out to be beneficial from a professional-development perspective. It provided a venue to associate with other CPA leaders across the state and talk strategies with those not in direct competition with us. I served on this committee for 15 years and met some great leaders in our profession.

I continued to multi-task with volunteerism, outside investing, and family involvement. There was never a time when I did not have plenty to do. I credit the busy schedule to forcing me to focus on the bigger decisions that would produce the greatest return. This helped me to obtain the best return on investment, ROI, of my time and money for the benefit of the firm.

My belief that perfection is a waste of time was extremely important. Some people get so involved in details they never get anything done. It is valuable to do a great job, but it is not necessary to dot every "I" and cross every "T." It still was about serving clients' needs and helping them meet their goals.

# CHAPTER 20:

*High-speed Decisions with Long-Term Results: Crucial for Business and Life*

Uneasiness began to grow within our firm around 1980. The principals were beginning to have differences of opinion on issues of proactive management versus reactive. We had grown too many junior partners too fast. They were talented professionals able to see greener pastures and looking to hang out their own shingles. Opportunities in the CPA profession were abundant. We had no restrictive competition agreements with employees.

The largest bomb in the history of our CPA firm was about to explode. My decision-making skills were about to be tested. My partners, Drake and Watters, suddenly and unexpectedly called a meeting in August of 1983 to announce they were leaving. Their new firm would be Drake, Watters & Company. Wanda Brieger would be joining them.

I was broadsided. Memories of events that washed over me during the next 30 days are still vivid in my mind. The three accountants proposed an option: they would retain the new office building and I would find new space; or, I would stay at 2545 Spring Arbor Road and they would move. Their plan was to be a buy-out of equity for the party that retained the building ownership. Our new building, occupied for just a few years, had debt and would be a heavy load of overhead for either party. I was not prepared to make that decision. The others had prepared for the separation and had an option on a new office location in the City of Jackson.

It was over. I had little time to do major thinking, evaluating, and forecasting once the departing partners made the announcement public. I knew getting upset would disturb me more than anyone else and I would not be able to think clearly. All parties agreed to remain calm and professional during this process. We vowed to work out a friendly and amicable settlement. I had to move quickly to evaluate my options, restructure and reorganize my business. So, I used the long-term decision-making process I developed and have advised clients to use over the years.

First, I reminded myself not to panic. Step two was to remember unemotional decisions provide the best results. Step three had me evaluate the situation and set a date for my decision. I called this my D-date. I reminded myself not to make decisions to appease people in the short term. The answer usually appeared clear the day before my target date. Using this process, I had time to think about all sides of the situation, consult with others if appropriate, and then decide on the best long-term solution. This planning process has proved successful for my clients and me time after time.

Another factor involved in my decision-making process was cost versus benefit. Here again, I did not let emotions drive my decision. I determined the cost and projected the future benefit. This strategy works on short or long-term decisions.

I also applied one of my favorite management tools, a daily to-do list that was prioritized with the most difficult and important tasks at the top. I got the tough jobs out of the way first, so they would not weigh on my thought processes throughout the day. This tool made the rest of my day easy for me. Too many people never get to the important and difficult jobs, tasks that continue to linger for days.

The item that topped my list during the pre-termination date with Drake & Watters was contacting key staff members and clients that may swing to either firm. I did that first, calling every client regardless of what I thought their answer would be. I counted only the "yes" answers because more often than not I received a "no." I wanted every one of them to know our firm would still be here to serve them if they needed us.

The largest decision was that of retaining our relatively new office building. I gave myself two weeks to make that decision. It took more than crunching numbers. There were so many unknowns ... the future number of employees ... the revenue that would continue. I used my best estimates with the confidence that the Willis firm would be successful in the long run. The answer to the major decision on the building was clear in my mind the day before my D-date.

The best long-term decision I made was to buy the building, assume the debt, and start rebuilding the firm. I knew we would have to make sacrifices in the short term but was confident in the long run we would fill the building. The location at 2545 Spring Arbor Road would be the place to be.

The belief that procrastination is a waste of time has long been one of my strengths in management. I gather the significant facts, make the decision, and move forward. The ironic part in making short-term decisions is that it does not make much difference in the end. It is the long-term decisions that are extremely important.

Drake & Watters had time to prepare and likely had done some grooming of significant clients in the process. They also had the advantage of working closely with many clients of the firm while I performed my activities inside and out of our business. I was the primary promoter of the firm in the community; the others focused more on delivering ongoing service. This gave them the advantage of recruiting the clients since they had more direct contact.

The even larger question in the equation was which firm the employees would elect to join. They had a choice to grow with either firm, rooting their decision on opportunity and management styles. I felt Drake & Watters had an advantage purely by the numbers and advance time of preparation. I had a tremendous amount of ground to cover with staffing and clients.

As time progressed, I realized there were only a few clients and staff faced with the difficult choice of which firm they would choose. Most of these people liked who they worked with and would stay the course with their primary service provider and associate at the firm. I decided I had to work on the key swing clients and staff and let the rest go. It was a difficult decision; they were all like family to me. I focused on those I could influence and hoped for the best.

I admit today to being disappointed when certain clients made their choice to go with Drake & Watters. I wished them well, avoided burning bridges and continued to be friends. We maintained mutual respect even though they did not use our services. A few eventually returned to our firm.

The employees that preferred the Drake & Watters' management style achieved their personal goals in a lower stress environment with good financial reward. I understood that people are born with different genes, raised in different environments, and choose the path that best meets their goals. They chose their business path and lived the lives they desired. Their path was successful for them. Our path proved successful for us.

There was one young CPA in the firm in whom both firms had an interest for future employment. Brian Jurasek interviewed with both parties a couple of times and decided to come with the future Willis & Willis CPA firm. His decision turned out to be beneficial to both of us as the firm now carries both names, Willis & Jurasek CPA's. Brian is living the dream I discussed with him in 1983. Today he is the lead owner and principal of the firm.

I felt in the long run our firm's management style would prevail. Some 30 years later, Willis & Jurasek, CPA's is the leading firm in the Jackson area. Drake & Watters sold their practice, closed their office and retired. All members of Willis & Jurasek, CPA's can be proud of creating a great organization that will carry on for years to come.

# CHAPTER 21:

## *Promoting Economic Development*

The conservative personal and business lifestyles of the principals of Willis, Drake & Watters had created options and future opportunities for us all. None of us had drained the company of cash flow to make payments on personal debts or other financial obligations. We had cash reserves. I had reduced my take home compensation over the years and now had the opportunity cash to invest in the future of Willis & Willis PC. I learned early on if I take care of my bread and butter business, this "Golden Goose" would take care of me, and it has.

We rattled around in the 6000-square-foot office space after the exit of almost half of the staff. I learned the hard way that working long hours and producing at 200% levels was not smart management. I now know a team approach can achieve much more for a business than that hard-working leader who does not utilize the assets of his crew.

I kept my office near the building's center to feel the firm's pulse. I was determined to be the confident leader who made sure each employee had an investment in the company's future. I gave our two key persons stock in the professional corporation and empowered them with leadership. Dennis C. Regan was our tax manager and the supporting person with the most experience. Brian Jurasek was the young motivated principal that I hoped would eventually lead the company. They each agreed our leadership format was to build a team that worked in harmony and utilized each person's strengths. We were determined not to form a firm of individuals.

Our people were to care for the clients they served like they cared for their own families. The Willis & Willis PC team responded. We serviced our clients, even communicating with them 24/7 if needed. Clients responded positively. I loved being able to pass compliments along from our clients to the service provider in our firm. We were all motivated by this positive atmosphere and were willing to contribute even more the next day.

Our bonus plan was structured so individuals were rewarded for their performance and the overall performance of the firm. Evaluation plans were established and monitored annually. This reward system was based on my philosophy that employees are number one. I have learned that if you take care of employees they will take care of the number two most important part of the equation: the customer or client.

We were meeting our goals. The business was growing. We were retaining reliable people. We were on budget. Warren Buffet would call our progress building intrinsic value. Another business guru might refer to as building goodwill. Whatever it was called, I knew that utilizing this competency in the business world would produce future cash flow. Generating cash flow and building value are fundamental to building a great business.

There were others who stood by me after the reorganization besides Regan and Jurasek. David Benson CPA, Constance Wortman, Deborah Westinghausen, and Lori Adair were hired out of high school or college. These lifers are still with us 30 years later. We work together and our families play together. Our team attracts new business because we are not just accountants and tax people. We are business consultants who help existing clients and new ones survive and thrive.

Our diversified client base was and still is the foundation on which we built our business. While Michigan was mired in the deepest recession since the Great Depression, our firm grew by evaluating the business market place, exploring area opportunities and seizing good clients.

I have shared with my clients and colleagues what my father taught me while duck hunting. Any hunter with common sense would prepare and plan before he pulled the trigger. The team at our firm used my Dad's logic every day as they worked with our clients. They did the research, helped clients prepare their vision, and then assisted them in carrying out their plan. We call this sound accounting practices.

After my father died, my mother's example taught my brother and me about hard work and perseverance. We could not sit back and wait for someone else to take care of us. Each of us had to pitch in and do the work. That wisdom has also been passed along through my colleagues to our clients.

# CHAPTER 22:

## Rebuilding the CPA Business

Back on the Intercostal Waterway in Florida, we were still waiting for the tow service to pull us out of the mud. Pat and I continued to examine the cause of our situation. Green and red channel markers bobbed in the water in every direction. How did boaters know where to go? There were markers coming in from the ocean and exiting to the west to the shipping yards. There were north and south markers on the Intercostal and its side channels. There were red markers and green markers and others with both green and red. We studied the paper chart and then *TransAction's* GPS screen. It appeared the fishing boat we were following left the Intercostal and headed down another channel that led to a marina.

When the towing service finally arrived, the captain threw lines to us and shouted instructions. He had us off in less than 15 minutes and then pulled up beside us to collect his well-earned fee. I handed over the cash and the freebooter gave me one of the broadest smiles I have ever seen, but no receipt. I do not like unexpected expenses on the first day of a trip. I do not like unexpected expenses, ever, but then sometimes you must pay the man. Before he left I confirmed directions north on the Intercostal, thanked him and we were off again.

Power Squadron training on Michigan's Great Lakes did not apply on Florida's Intercostal Waterway. We recognized the Intercostal had its own set of rules when it comes to red and green markers. The red markers were always on the U.S. mainland side of the channel. Pat and I were getting on-the-job training in unpredictable rule changes, an unexpected silver lining we would use in business ventures and our future boating adventures.

My accounting career began with an unpredictable obstacle more substantial than being stuck on a sand bar. Michigan was in a serious recession in the mid-1980s. Clients were closing their doors. Major employers were moving Michigan operations south. Jackson County alone had three vital business closings in two years.

The first to announce it was closing was Clark Equipment. The company-built forklift-trucks and employed 2,700 workers. It was 1982. Shortly after Clark, Goodyear Tire announced they were closing their Jackson operations. The tire company employed 1,000. The following year Walker Manufacturing, now Tenneco, announced they were ending their muffler manufacturing division. Several hundred employees were left without work.

Most people are familiar with the general equation that one manufacturing job creates an additional seven supporting jobs in any given community. Jackson County was relatively small at that time with about 70,000 jobs for a population of 150,000. The ripple effect of the three closings reduced the workforce by more than 10 percent and was further compounded by the announced closing of the Commonwealth Engineering Company in 1985.

Commonwealth employed 2,700 including professional engineers whose primary focus was engineering nuclear power plants. Early in the '80s legislators and environmentalists decided nuclear power plants were dangerous and ended new construction in the United States. Commonwealth began layoffs and was eventually sold around 1990. The Michigan economy had hit the bottom.

The Jackson Alliance for Business Development, or JABD, had been formed in the early '80s to retain area companies and attract new ones. Their mission was to help businesses comply with the laws, regulations, and ordinances that slowed their development. I was asked to join the group as a director. I jumped at the chance to lend a hand at digging Jackson's economy out of the hole. But board members didn't operate as forward thinkers or entrepreneurs. The organization was slow to react. The chair and vice-chair had terminated employees and were about to reduce operations to a couple of hours per week. They were working on a plan to contract out services.

Traveling around the State I observed how communities dealt with retaining existing business and attracting new. I checked back at our Jackson office. Several weeks had passed with no additional information on the service plan. It was time to act.

I called a special meeting of the board and the stakeholders-the governmental agencies, and businesses in the community that funded the operations. We asked the chair and vice-chair to explain their actions and present their plan. Their response was weak. After considerable discussion few answers and no definite plans for the future surfaced. Not one of the talented people sitting around that table could see how to dig the Alliance out of that hole. It was so exasperating, and I was so determined to bring about change in the organization and our community that I pounded the table and demanded a plan. I do not recall any time in my life being so inspired for action as at that moment. Despite my inspiration, the meeting ended without a plan.

I called another board meeting for reorganization after the chair and vice-chair resigned. Following a long discussion, I agreed to chair the group. The JABD rehired part of the staff and reorganized. I could see our staff was spending an inordinate amount of time doing bookkeeping and administrative work instead of working on economic development.

I had heard of privately organized groups that connected inventors with entrepreneurs in my travels around the state. I did some investigation, spoke with community leaders and determined there was enough support in Jackson County to organize a board and adopt a mission for such an agency. We called the organization the Jackson Venture Capital Group, or JVCG. Our mission was to provide a forum for inventors and entrepreneurs to meet and develop new businesses for Jackson County. Jobs would be the byproduct.

I was totally taken off guard when I entered the venue that first evening. There were presenters of every kind from all over Michigan. How they found out about us was a mystery to me. I was nearly in tears when I stepped up to the podium in front of almost 200 people as chair of the JVCG and introduced 20 entrepreneurs to present to the group of investors. I encouraged both groups to meet following the formal presentations. Following that seminal event, the JVCG board held weekly breakfast meetings to lay plans for future forums and provide further assistance in building relationships between investors and entrepreneurs.

Between 1986 and 2000, some of the darkest years in Michigan's economy, the JVCG provided a forum for entrepreneurs and investors, an opportunity for them to infuse capital into several existing businesses and start 35 new ones.

# CHAPTER 23:

## *Know When to Ask for Help*

Michigan was playing at the Rose Bowl! The game started at five o'clock. We had a big night planned with our friends, Kirk and Marty Mercer. They were waiting for us to dock *TransAction* at Stuart. We would be joining them to watch the game. We were off the sandbar and off our schedule. As we motored up the Intercostal waterway we were anxious, afraid we might not arrive in time to watch the game.

We were stunned when we entered the large bay at Stuart. The number of multi-colored buoys bobbing in the bay amid boats cruising in every direction was unlike any situation we had encountered while boating in Michigan's Great Lakes or protocol covered in Power Squadron training. Channel markers identified shallow reefs. That we knew. But we were still gun-shy about running aground especially since it would involve missing the most important football game of the year. We knew from business dealings to ask for help when stuck, so I made a cell phone call to our friends.

Kirk offered to send a boat out to guide us into the marina, and in the chaos of the moment, we accepted. It didn't take long to follow the boat through the maze and moor our vessel at the marina. We met our friends, had a good meal and were in time to enjoy the game. The Mercers came aboard early the next morning. *TransAction* headed for Lake Okeechobee, a route that we knew required some risk.

Warren Buffet says risk comes from not knowing what you're doing. I studied my charts the night before we struck out for the new adventure. They indicated our route wound through rivers with swift currents and required us to clear a couple of locks. My crew agreed to help. Together we guided *TransAction* up the serpentine waterway without incident. When we entered the fresh water lake the surrounding countryside was billowing smoke from local farmers burning sugarcane stalks. The black ash drifted down on *TransAction's* white deck and required extra scrubbing by my crew when we reached the dock. We moored at the marina owned by the fisherman Roland Martin of television fame. The slip we picked was close to a saloon where beer bottles lined the bar and the fish stories of the day had already begun. We uncapped a couple ourselves as happy hour began.

Navigating a vessel like *TransAction* involves risk. It takes a high level of focus, and plenty of preparation, a lot like a business venture. I follow my own strict code of never drinking alcohol until we are docked. When we have completed a successful docking at the end of the day our custom is to celebrate by uncapping a beer. I like to think of it as a Willis tradition. We have never had an unsuccessful docking, so I guess that means we celebrate after every day trip.

# CHAPTER 24:

## *Alternative Financing*

Boating in waters with changing rules reminded me of the State of Michigan's guidelines during the economic downturn in the late 1980s. Our economy in Jackson County was stagnant. An effort to offer an alternative financing vehicle, a Business Industrial Development Corporation, or BIDCO, was being led Dean Edwards, CEO of Midwest Bank.

BIDCOs were already being approved and licensed by the State of Michigan. The idea was that the state would invest 50 cents for every dollar of private capital raised once the BIDCO license was approved. The Dean Edwards Group, had a strong team and even as we were denied approval for licensing, followed the guidelines.

Members of the Jackson Venture Capital Group, the JVCG, attempted to pick up where the Edwards Group left off, and provide mezzanine financing on collateral for medium-sized business with a focus on the Jackson area. The in-between stance for a BIDCO would be that banks would take the low risk, BIDCO's mezzanine plan would take a greater risk and the owners would take the maximum risk.

I met Patricia Machnik, a recently divorced, former middle school teacher who had made a career change and became a licensed securities broker/advisor. She was working as a commercial loan officer at Security Savings and Loan. We had been discussing the BIDCO opportunity and building a management team, an effort that would involve some of the JVCG board and other community leaders. Pat's employer learned of Pat's involvement with BIDCO and terminated her on the spot. That was not good for Pat who was a single mother with limited funds.

The Dean Edwards group had been turned down. They had a good plan and an excellent team. What were our chances? Pat and I knew we had to pursue it on our personal time and that it would be a major commitment. We leaned heavily on the resources of the Willis & Willis CPA firm. Discussions led to dating, and dating led to Pat becoming my wife.

Our group applied to the State of Michigan for a license. Officials advised us the approval process would take a year with no guarantee. A detailed business plan and ten years of financial projections were required along with a third person with extensive business/banking experience. Robert Ballentine was recently retired from Comerica Bank. We asked him to join us and be the president of Jackson BIDCO.

With Ballentine in the lead position, we developed plans and forecasts and held monthly half-day meetings in Lansing with State administrators of Economic

Development for the BIDCO program. We built a board of folks with a passion for economic development, people who were able to invest and had contacts who might also be willing to invest. Raising $3,000,000 in private investment money for an unknown start-up company turned out to be one heck of a challenge, but not nearly as much of a challenge as we received from the State of Michigan administrators who sent us home again to rewrite our plan and projections.

The government's requests seemed repetitive and unreasonable. That division of the bureaucracy had approved only four BIDCOs in the two years they had been operating. Nearly a year had passed since our initial application and the powers in Lansing were giving us no assurance we would get a license. Most start-ups would have quit by now, but we could see the potential for the community, and continued with the process.

Although we had raised some seed money, I was funding most of the start-up costs. The board of directors approved the hiring of Pat full-time on a meager salary of $2,000 a month. She would not have been able to make it without some support from her mother, Marie Hewitt. Pat could have returned to teaching, but she now had it in her blood to enter the business field. It was a rough and tumble start but she said she was determined to make it work.

One of our first recruits for the new BIDCO board was Walter Boris, a retired executive of Consumers Power. Walt had been a high-powered senior manager of this

SEC public company based in Jackson and was loaded with top-level finance experience. He also had a great sense of humor. His management skills and commitment to form a BIDCO made Walt's move into the position of chairman seamless. We loved Walt's Golden Rule: Those with the gold rule.

Our plan took a detour when the personal plans of Robert Ballentine changed. He withdrew from being our initial CEO. Our statewide search for a replacement ended in Ann Arbor, a college town about 35 miles to the east of Jackson. Raymond Waters had been involved in the management of his in-law's auto dealerships in the state of Wyoming before returning to Ann Arbor. He agreed to accept the position of CEO without compensation until the BIDCO was approved, licensed, and we had raised our capital.

The application process continued with the state for another six months. During that period Michigan had approved one more BIDCO. Many applicants had fallen by the wayside and the odds were looking slim for us. Following the formal procedures of the next monthly meeting, I called a side meeting with the head of the department. My goal was to add pressure. We had nothing to lose. I told him he had two weeks to approve or disapprove our application. I wanted a "yes" or "no" answer. The man was startled by my bluntness and said he would let us know. I repeated my demands and said, "Two weeks. That is, it." Within two weeks, our answer came. We were approved.

The next step was for Jack Schomer to prepare an Offering Memorandum. Jack was our legal counsel and assisted in raising capital. We set a date and money goal and went to work raising the capital. I made a significant pledge up front to show my commitment. We targeted venture capitalists and anyone with a passion for the financial growth of the community. We learned to accept the "NO" word along the path. It was not uncommon for Ray, Pat, and I to have eight to ten meetings a week laying plans and requesting money. We kept marching forward and made our $3,000,000 goal within our timeframe.

During the next ten years Jackson BIDCO funded 40 companies across the State including some of Michigan's fastest growing businesses. We had created an imprint as being a leader in the financing and private equity area. Our management team consulted and met with client companies on a regular basis. We offered suggestions and guidance but declined serving on their boards. The fastest growing companies unfortunately did not always turn out to be the most successful. Their business plans were often focused more on growth than on the bottom line. We had formed the BIDCO in a time when banks were not extending credit in the business sector, providing significant help in those difficult times. Jackson BIDCO, later renamed Horizon BIDCO, ran its course near the end of the decade.

Banks were now making loans to companies that Horizon BIDCO had turned down and denied credit. We entered into an orderly liquidation as we continued to observe the banks filling the credit gap. This was the beginning of a new era when banks began to make high-risk loans to unqualified companies. It was the beginning of the national and world credit crisis that peaked in 2008 and 2009.

The orderly liquidation of Horizon BIDCO was completed in two years and we returned the investors' money in full with a small return. Pat entered the investment advisor field full time with her own company. Ray went to work for the community development fund in Detroit, and I continued with Willis & Willis PC and my projects.

# CHAPTER 25:

## *Choosing the Right Partner*

Tom Trosin had a work ethic like no one else I have ever met. He didn't grow up working on a farm like I did. He learned from his parents while growing up in in Fort Wayne, Indiana.

Our story together began in the late '80s with two Jackson clients of my CPA firm. They both owned separate businesses in a building they co-owned. To complicate matters further, both clients were 50 percent owners of each other's corporations, an unusual business plan I would not recommend. Lee Blake Precision Machining was a profitable computer numerically controlled, CNC, business managed by Partner "A." Micro Form was profitable enough to pay its manager, Partner "B," an excellent salary. It was a formed tool business located on the opposite end of the building.

The trouble started when the CNC business became substantially more profitable and Partner "A" had to share profits with Partner "B." Jealousies began to brew when the CNC business moved to a new facility. Partner "B," still a 50% owner of the building and the CNC business, was dissatisfied with the situation. After multiple discussions, the two owners could not reach an agreement.

I could see the problem. A 50-50 partnership gives neither party control of the shareholder voting process to make change. So, when there's a stalemate, either both partners agree to sell everything and renegotiate the 50-50 arrangement, or one party takes legal action in the court system, and the judge and jury decide what's fair.

A court settlement can be an ugly and expensive way to settle a dispute. Stress and grief caused by the legal process usually take their toll on all parties in situations like this, and in the meantime the value of the business declines. The legal process could take as long as two years to settle with the biggest winners usually being attorneys.

Another reason to avoid the court system is that generally the judge and jury members do not grasp the nature of the business nor the valuation process. They do not understand cash flow and what it takes to run a business. How many savvy business people do you suppose would be on any given jury? The judge and jurors hear excerpts from the depositions of all parties involved. Often, statements in the trial are taken out of context. Attorneys and the witnesses often create mass confusion in trying to prove their case. Sometimes the chaos is accidental. Sometimes it's intentional. You never know what the verdict will be.

I was once a witness in a case of a business valuation in a divorce proceeding. In my opinion, the judge came in with an unrealistically high valuation for the business. He ruled that the business owner had to make payments to the former spouse out of cash flow over an 18-month period. The problem was that if all went well in the business, it would take up to 10 years to generate that much cash flow. I am not sure on the outcome, but I was confident that the court's decision would not work.

The disagreement between Micro Form and Lee Blake Precision resolved when Partners "A" and "B," both educated and intelligent individuals, decided to cash out and sell both businesses. Their goal was to maximize their money and each start over.

Since I was the CPA for both companies, the two gentlemen came to me and asked if I knew of any potential buyers. I had referred clients and business people to prospects in the past and facilitated many successful deals. The benefit to me was that I created good business relationships from these referrals and many times continued or created a new business client for our CPA firm.

I left the meeting that day thinking about prospects for the businesses and seeing a potential opportunity for a good investment. I began thinking about how I could put together a team that could provide both capital and management.

I made some inquiries and was directed to Tom Trosin, who was now living and working in Jackson. I remember playing golf with Tom at Arbor Hills Country Club where he won the 9-hole match play. He was about 6-foot-5 and had a great personality. At 5-foot-8, I looked like a dwarf standing next to this giant of a man. My most vivid memory of the game is the score he took on the eighth hole. He hit the ball from one sand trap to another. He finally recorded a 14 on the par 4. I felt sorry for the poor guy, but he laughed it off and did not seem to get frustrated. "I need to practice my wedge shots" was all he said. That's the kind of person you want as a partner. If he had thrown his club and started cussing a blue streak, we would not have become business associates or friends.

I have found that when selecting a business partner or a partner to marry, many of the same attributes apply. First, you need to have trust and respect for one another. You need to be able to sit down and talk things out with open minds. You must be able to express your feelings and get everything out on the table for discussion and debate. You need to reach decisions with compromise, and trust that the other party means his or her best and will carry it out. You should not look back at the past and criticize each other for what was not done. You look at the past to guide you in decision-making, yes, but it's the present and the future that count. It's in the present that you can make good decisions.

I like and respect Warren Buffet of Berkshire Hathaway. His belief in trusting the competence of his managers has made him one of the richest people in the world. He is modest and does not brag about his wealth. He thanks his team and encourages them to continue their efforts to build more successful divisions. In addition, he is an extremely giving person. Taking the lowest salary of any Wall Street executive, he gets paid with the success of the team and the company. I hadn't heard of Warren Buffet when I started out in business, but by the late 1990s had purchased stock in his company and have been rewarded with great returns ever since.

Tom Trosin graduated from Indiana University and is an understated kind of guy, a lot like Warren Buffet. He started his career with Ford Motor Company in Dearborn and ended up in Jackson managing a plant for SOS Consolidated. Labor unions were near their peak at the time. Tom de-unionized the plant after some bitter relationships and set a high standard for productivity. I held several meetings with Tom regarding Lee Blake until he finally said, "You put the deal together and I'll run it."

Negotiations began with the owners and continued for some time. The United States economy was experiencing 15% inflation in the early 1980s and the prime interest rate charged by the banks was 20%. The challenges were to arrive at an acceptable price and to figure out how to finance the purchase.

Initially, we were going to have three partners, but one decided not to participate. I gave Tom the first option to buy out that third partner. He accepted. We reached an agreement on the price with the owners. The sellers consented to a 39% down payment and were willing to finance the balance. Payments were to be short-term, based on a 5-year amortization. We closed the sale and took over the companies in 1980.

Interest rates generally rise and fall with inflation and there are several impacting factors. It's a complicated issue, but basically inflation increases when the demand for goods exceeds supply. A recent example is in the housing industry in the early 2000s. Cheap money from bad and fraudulent loans drove up housing prices at an unrealistic rate causing inflation in that industry. In the case of the housing matter, this was created by too much borrowing or debt.

The major cause of inflation in the 1970s and early '80s was the result of our imported oil prices. It drove up the cost of everything from transportation to food prices, since food must be transported from the farm to the dinner table. When that happens, inflation then becomes psychological and prices rise in the entire market place. Employees want more compensation to keep up with the growing costs, which further increases the ripple effect throughout the whole economy.

I look back today and think that it was a courageous decision at the time for Tom and me to purchase the business. We were both entrepreneurs and not opposed to taking calculated risks in making business decisions. We understood the sacrifices owners may have to take as being an investment in the company's future. We knew we could not expect compensation or benefits during the tough times.

Tom was prepared to take over operations as president of the company the day after we sealed the deal. It was his first opportunity to be the leader and he was quite comfortable. Partner "A" assisted in the transition of customers and employees. We had about ten employees at that time. Partner "A" moved to California after the sale and started a similar CNC machine business. Partner "B" moved to Florida and invested in real estate. They were both successful.

# CHAPTER 26:

*Still Tougher Times Can Make*
*Friends for Life*

All was going well in the Michigan economy when our business started out. Then suddenly in 1982, the wheels came off the manufacturing industry in the State. Michigan and other northern states became known as the rust belt because it was a high-cost place to do business. Companies moved their jobs to the southern states where they could find incentives for new plants with cheap labor, plus additional benefits.

Tom and I knew we were in a recession when our primary customer, Aeroquip, cut their orders and we began to have major cash flow problems. He agreed to reduce his salary and later eliminated his salary for a period to give the business a chance to survive. Tom exceeded my expectations as a leader and shared my motto, "Do your share and a little bit more."

Tom and I both knew to keep personal living expenses under control, so they would not become a burden to the business. We both knew of businessmen who lost everything because they were determined to continue their salaries and fringe benefits and maintain their standard of living during the recession.

My father, grandfather and even my great-grandfather would agree it's not prudent to spend money before you have it, or to live above your means. Even if you can afford certain luxuries, it behooves you to keep an eye on your personal cash flow and opportunity money. The person's business is the proverbial Golden Goose. Taking out too much money will kill the goose that lays the golden egg. I believe 50% of business failures could be avoided if the owners had not killed the Goose with cash withdrawals to maintain a certain life style.

Our story at Lee Blake Precision Machining is a successful one because of the sacrifices and extraordinary efforts Tom made to recharge the business. He did not sit back and wait for things to happen. Tom made things happen.

The president of our company turned on his sales charm and began pounding the pavement for new customers. Tom knew the medical business was doing well and drove to Kalamazoo to approach Stryker Corp, an up-and-coming medical manufacturer, now one of the world leaders in artificial joints. He managed to make his way into the company's purchasing department, which I am sure was no small challenge. He must have heard "no" a few times, but he was resilient. Tom was able to see the purchasing agent and asked for work. She showed him several parts drawings and asked him if Lee Blake could make any of them. Tom responded, "We can make them all, but give me the most complicated part required for your manufacturing process."

Part manufactured by Lee Blake Precision

She handed the part and drawing to Tom, and he headed back to Jackson. He needed to impress this buyer. The next morning, he returned to Stryker carrying the precious parts, products of Tom and his head machinists working all night. Stryker tested the parts. They met all the company's high standards. The orders began to flow, and Tom saved Lee Blake.

It took extraordinary sacrifice and effort to save the company. But hard work was only the beginning. It took creative thinking and effort as well. Who else would have returned the very next morning with the parts for

Stryker? Because Tom did, he got the purchase order. A quality product with service exceeding customer expectations, is a winning combination.

Lee Blake started on an upward sales spiral when many other businesses around us were failing. We outgrew our building and purchased a new facility. Tom preformed every role from sales to plant manager. His goal was to keep overhead low. He was working such long hours he could have died doing so much, so I encouraged him to hire a plant manager. He was reluctant at first but later told me he was relieved to give up that responsibility. Tom kept his finger on the pulse of every phase of the operation.

The man was also a great team builder. He generated high morale in the business with various rewards for the employees. One idea he implemented was "Beer Friday." The employees were rewarded with an early Friday closing and some kegs of beer. Being a hands-on manager, Tom organized and planned most of these events himself. One of the incentive gifts was the Lee Blake jacket, meant to show the community that they were proud to work at Lee Blake. He always looked for ways to encourage the employees to take pride in the company and in their work.

Tom also created marketing gifts for clients. He was an all-around businessman and promoter. He came up with a clock as a customer gift idea. The motto on the clock was "Never too late; call Lee Blake." That was synonymous with Tom's desire that no order came in too late in the day. Lee Blake accepted all orders and delivered the parts the next day. Additionally, the order would be delivered with precision and quality with the goal of exceeding customer expectations. The procedures and incentives proved to be successful and the company continued to grow in all departments.

Lee Blake had grown to 50 employees with two shifts. Sometimes business and personnel issues would get to Tom since he wanted to handle all these matters himself. The man never stopped; he was the original Energizer Bunny. I encouraged him to hire an operations person, so he could focus on sales and be a managing president. We searched but never found one. Tom was wearing out. We had been in business almost seven years and he was managing all operations of the company, a monumental job.

I like to encourage numerous meetings with my business associates in a fun and relaxed environment. Tom and I had many good times together, looking at expansion opportunities or ways to promote the business. Open discussions in a relaxed environment with a beer or two can work great.

Tom called me one day and asked if we could meet for lunch. He usually began our times together with a story or joke. Some were favorites of his that I had heard before. But we always got a good laugh out of them whether I had heard them before or not. This time Tom opened the discussion with a new subject. Tom Trosin wanted to sell the business and he said he had a buyer. I was surprised, but after further discussion it all began to make sense.

We would sell Lee Blake to Melling Tool. Tom would work for the company as VP of sales. I never debated the issue and agreed with his decision if the price was reasonable and the agreement with his new employer-to-be was at arm's length and not influenced by the sale.

We discussed what Lee Blake Precision Machining was worth. I have a philosophy that cash flow drives the value of the business. I recommend to my clients that they use a multiple of five to seven times cash flow when purchasing a business. The price or value of the business for me is not five times earnings but five times cash flow.

Cash flow is the cash available after all expenses, but before payments of a long-term debt. I like to see a business paid for in five to seven years after purchase. This principal was applied to the Lee Blake purchase. We as sellers, had excellent cash flow. We used a multiple of five.

Potential earning power based on many factors will also affect the value. This is more difficult to predict. If you look at several years of company records and see that the cash flow is rising, you may sell your business for up to 10 times the previous year's net cash flow. If cash flow has declined steadily for several years, your business value will be liquidation value or auction value.

Tom brought up the idea of a cash offer. I told him I wanted to look at our numbers and see if the price fit in the range of my valuation formula. I crunched the numbers of Lee Blake and agreed that the offering price was within my valuation formula, five to seven times annual cash flow. The next step was to have the legal documents prepared to close the sale. We closed, and the deal was paid for within 30 days, extremely fast considering the dollars involved. It turns out Tom was well rewarded for taking the risk of owning two thirds of Lee Blake Machining.

Tom's experience with Melling has been rewarding for him and for them. He has managed and guided Melling Tool to several successful acquisitions and operating improvements throughout the world. Presently responsible for several divisions and well beyond retirement, Tom is still motivated and stays active. We both believe that being active is healthy for the mind and body. It keeps the brain churning and the opportunities flowing.

Tom and I continue to get together and enjoy each other's company. We have completed a few subsequent partnerships with moderate success and will keep making deals as long as we live.

I have learned that if you like your partners enough to be close friends, and if you keep an open mind and an open heart leaving unnecessary ego out of the equation, you can have meaningful, profitable, and lasting relationships. I have learned not to get involved in business with someone with whom you would not share a meal, join for a hunting or fishing trip, or play a round of golf.

# CHAPTER 27:

## *The Balanced Life*

The author Robert Fulgham said it best: "Be aware of wonder. Live a balanced life – learn some and think some...and play and work every day some."

While Pat and I were dating, I invited her to go cross-country skiing with me in an 80-acre parcel owned by my family. The property stayed flooded year around and was heavily covered with tamarack trees. It could only be traversed in the winter when the ground was frozen. I did not mention to her that the area was untraveled. Even though this property had been in the family for 60 years, this was my first time to explore this area. We ducked under branches and squeezed between trees for about 20 minutes when Pat said she'd had enough and wanted to go back to the truck. I pointed her in the direction of my vehicle and continued, searching for high ground where deer might hide out.

I never did find the high ground or the deer. When I finally returned to the truck, I didn't find Pat either. I started the diesel, honked the horn, and called out her name. No answer. I knew she was lost. I drove the perimeter of the area, honking and calling. Still no answer.

I drove to the farmhouse to see if she was there, but no Pat. My heart sank. I remember hearing stories about thin ice near Goose Lake that adjoins our tamarack swamp. Goose Lake is where "Michigan's Woodstock" took place in 1970, drawing nearly 200,000 members of the youth counterculture from all over the country. I returned to the 80-acre parcel, honking and calling for her, but still no response. It was time to dial 911 and get help. This was in 1988 before cell phones. I had to drive back to the farmhouse to make the call.

When I entered, there was Pat, baking brownies in the kitchen. I didn't know whether to yell at her or hug her. I settled on a hug. She went on to describe her return trip, which involved getting lost and being chased by a bull. Needless to say, we both got plenty of exercise that day.

I have always loved Northern Michigan. Years later, Pat and I rented condo units for three years on Clam Lake from our friends Jack and Sharon Mallow. One day Jack said, "I have had those damn condos for sale for a year and can't sell them." He told me he was tired of paying dues and property taxes for units he didn't use.

"You did not tell me you had them for sale," I said. Jack told me the price and Pat and I bought them. After receiving considerable advice from the seller, Pat and I arrived at our remodeling plan and proceeded.

"Up North" adventures were made into memories for us, our children and our grandkids over the next 20 years: Josh climbing a tree and falling into the lake, all of us dropping stones off the bridge on the way to Butchers', playing with lake toys in the low rent district of Torch lake, the portage to Traverse Bay and Lake Michigan, the afternoons socializing on the sandbar of Torch Lake, the fireworks, the long, peaceful days, the fishing with the Mickey Mouse pole off the dock with the children's hooks catching dock posts, Pat's shirt and Marie's shoe, the grandkids catching a perch, hooking it on as bait and landing a pike as long as the fishing rod, the visits to small towns like Alden and Bellaire, the meals at the Dockside, Lulus, the Shorts Brewery, Toonies, Kathy's Kitchen, and the Lamp Lighter Inn, the visit by the Sheriff to the dock on July 4th to check our boat registration that was left in the 'up north box' back in Jackson, the swans eating chips and chasing our jet skis, the ducks, the mink playing on the dock, the winter ice and mountains of snow, Caitlin training to ski at Schuss and Boyne Mountain, the snowboarding, Jamie saying, "I tried to stop, but couldn't," the flexible bones and finally the broken arm. These memories will someday become our family's legends.

We all enjoyed sleeping "Up North," and taking long walks in the late morning to inhale the fresh air and the smell of pine trees. We usually visited Butch's Tackle and Party Store and stopped at the top of the bridge over Clam River to watch fish, swans, geese and ducks floating in the fast-moving water entering Torch Lake. We never crossed the bridge without Caitlin throwing pebbles in the river. Five-year old Jamie referred to Butch's Tackle as Butchers, and often asked, "When can we go to Butchers?" From then on it became known to all of us as "Butchers." The adventures "Up North" were never complete until each of us threw a few stones and pebbles from the bridge.

When Pat and I purchased the condos, we intended their use be year-around, and it was. In the summer we enjoyed boating. Autumns "Up North" were beautiful for watching the leaves turn colors. And in the winter months we enjoyed skiing and snowmobiling.

Scott & Josh Willis "Up North"

Pat "Up North"

Phil "Up North"

Our grandchildren joined us on snow ski trips to Schuss Mountain, Shanty Creek, and Boyne Mountain, all less than an hour drive from the condos. Some of them starting skiing as young as three. Once they learned the ropes, it was difficult to keep them off the slopes. They'd cry at the end of the day when we asked them, "Aren't you freezing cold?" They would respond, "Yes, but we don't want to go home."

I took Josh to Boyne Mountain to test his skills at the advanced snowboarding park. It was late in March, a beautiful spring day for snowboarding. The day was going well until it was time to go back to the condo. Josh wanted to go down one more time. I could see he was tired, and I was too. He insisted he was up for one more trip down the slope, and off we went. Josh took off fast advancing toward the first rail in the park. His board caught the edge of the rail. He bounced off and landed about ten feet below, head first on the hard-packed snow.

I was anxious. He was not wearing a helmet. I rushed to his side. Josh lay moaning. He eventually began to move around and finally sat up. We talked awhile until he said he was ready to go. We rode the boards to the bottom of the slope and I immediately purchased a helmet for him. That was a valuable lesson for Josh about preparation and knowing his limits, and a reminder for me of what my mother said about protecting my health. "Nothing else in life means much if you do not have good health."

When my step-grandson Ethan Ray joined us in later years, he did not want to mess around with skis and took up snowboarding. One day he gathered the family for an exhibition to show his progress at the snowboarding park at Schuss Mountain. He shot down the slope heading for the first rail at a speed greatly exceeding his ability. He took the rail as any Olympic boarder would do but sailed through the air out of control landing hard on the snowpack below. We rushed to the scene to see if he was okay. His body was bruised but not as much as his pride. I give Ethan credit. He has continued to advance his snowboarding skills and now enjoys the sport with his friends at resorts around the state of Michigan. There is nothing more important than the kind of perseverance Ethan displayed.

As the children and grandchildren matured, the coordination of family trips became difficult, and we each embraced other activities. Fond memories of our "Up North" experiences will remain with all of us. We sold the condos in 2014 after 20 wonderful years in the Torch Lake area. This time the timing was right for the sale of our real estate, unlike my earlier Farwell Lake venture. Our return on investment matched my best business models, doubling at the time of sale.

# CHAPTER 28:

## *Living the Nightmare*

Early one January morning in 2005 I was working out in our gym at our home on Brown's Lake. Pat was getting ready to go to the club gym for her work out, but before she left at 6:30, she commented, "Something smells funny" I told her we have new paint, new stain, and new lumber in the house and that is most likely what she smelled. She shrugged her shoulders, gave me a kiss, and took off for the club. I continued my workout, went to the kitchen for a glass of orange juice and then to our bathroom to shower. When I stepped out of the shower, I smelled something unusual. I smelled smoke!

I wrapped myself in a towel and began to search our home. When I got to the living room, I spotted ringlets of smoke in the air. I knew this was serious and beyond what a home extinguisher could accomplish, so I picked up the house phone and hit 911. The phone was dead.

I grabbed my cell phone. Again, I hit 911. It rang several times, but there was no answer. I ran back upstairs and pulled on a pair of jeans, t-shirt, and sweatshirt. There was no time for socks, so I just stepped into my shoes. I went out to my car, which had a different cell phone line. The no-service indicator was showing. "Oh, my God," I thought as I walked through the 6-inch snow, first to one neighbor's home and then another's. I pounded on the doors and yelled, "Help!" No one answered at either house. Fifteen minutes had passed since my initial conversation with Pat, but it seemed like a lifetime.

I ran back into our house to use the first cell phone to call my office. I tried different lines. "Come on, answer; please, someone answer." Christine Ward, our audit manager, picked up her line. "Thank God, you're there!" I yelled into the phone. "Call 9-1-1 and send them to my house." I gave her my address just to be sure she had it. I backed my car out of the garage and closed the door to reduce the oxygen available to stoke the fire. Waiting anxiously for the fire department to arrive, I tried calling Pat, but, of course, she didn't answer because she was exercising. She always leaves her phone in the car while she works out.

Somehow, I had the presence of mind to know this was out of my control. I stood outside in the snow, watched and waited. The fire trucks arrived in a few minutes. When the firemen went through the garage and opened the house, thick black smoke billowed out. One of them asked me if I knew where the fire might have started. Based on my quick search earlier, it appeared that the bulk of the smoke had been on the east end of the first floor.

I stood outside with the fire chief listening to his conversation on his two-way radio with two firemen who entered the house. They searched the kitchen first, and then ruled it out. They climbed the stairs to a second-floor bedroom instead of where I had said I'd seen the smoke. I kept repeating, "It started downstairs."

Sometime later, the chief began to act nervously. He said that one of his men was out of oxygen and the two firemen were buddy breathing, taking turns with one oxygen tank. We could see their figures through the bedroom window. I felt some relief. I assumed the firefighters on the ground would set up a ladder and the men would exit. But to our surprise, the men inside disappeared.

We didn't know it. None of us could see it. The southeast corner of my home was engulfed in flames. I heard the fire chief say, "We've got a problem. Fireman down." By now, seven fire departments from nearby townships, three police cars, and an ambulance swarmed onto the property.

Fire fighters hosed down the west end of the house with chemicals and water to try and save the firemen. The flames continued to rage out-of-control, consuming the rest of our home. The fire chief got word the downed fireman was located. Two firefighters broke out the lakeside window, went inside, and lowered the man to the ground.

All of this happened while Pat was at the club. When she arrived home, she saw the commotion and assumed it was the neighbor's home, since trucks were parked there as well. When she made her way to the front of where our house once stood, I hugged her.

Two hours later, the firefighters were still working to put out the fire. When the smoke finally subsided, we learned that one of the firefighters had died. Our family and the entire community were devastated by the loss of this 19-year veteran firefighter. Well-liked by many, he was also a state-certified instructor and had trained many of his colleagues who deeply respected his abilities. Married with two young children, his was the first death of a fireman in our county in 23 years.

# CHAPTER 29:

## *He Was So Young*

The afternoon of the fire, Carolyn, my former wife who lived nearby, invited us over to rest and have some hot soup. The high temperature that day was 20 degrees. Before we went to Carolyn's, Pat and I sat in our car near the pile of rubble and looked on as investigators looked through the ashes for answers. We were numb. A man had died in our home trying to save our belongings. It was a hard fact to process. His wife. His children. His age.

We ate Carolyn's soup in silence, rested and then returned to the site. The ashes and debris from the basement had been spread all over the property by a huge hydro hoe to allow the hot coals to cool.

There were so many things that had gone wrong that day, but I am most grateful we are alive. We could have both died in our sleep had the fire started during the night. I am so grateful for our dear friends. Forty-to-fifty people called to invite us to stay in their homes when they heard the news. One of those friends, James Bailey, called three times. Eventually, we rented the fully furnished home of his then future wife, Melissa.

The next weeks were challenging, to say the least. The print and local TV media were intrusive, running the story for six straight days. We asked for a break, but the requests for interviews continued. What could we say? We were all running on empty. Both the firemen's and my family were hurting. We got to know the fireman's widow and set up a funded scholarship for the children.

We found out what it was like to have nothing. The evening of the fire, we shopped for essentials. For the first two weeks, we stayed with our friends Ed and Marie Machnik while we began to assess the process of getting our lives back.

While smoke continued to rise from the remains of the structure, family members helped me rake through ashes to try to salvage anything that was not destroyed. One outer garage had survived the fire, so we began stashing things we found in there. Pat could not imagine why or what I was going to do with what she referred to as "that junk," but it was not junk to me. It was my family history held in the lost heirlooms.

We found pieces from two family antique table settings, a centennial settee, and two valuable antique quilts on the floor of where a closet in the west end of our home was still partially standing. One of the quilts was identified as having been made in 1897 by Kate Willis, my great-aunt.

Shortly after this hunt for treasures the remaining brick walls and concrete chimney structure were knocked into the basement for safety reasons. The next morning, we arrived to see three inches of snow had covered the scene, making it look and feel pure again.

We had a difficult time sleeping at all. We were dealing with stress for weeks following the fire. We needed a new wardrobe, a place to live and to decide about rebuilding a new home. Through it all we continued counted our blessings and keeping our thoughts and minds positive as family and many loving friends surrounded and supported us.

I drove to the burn site during lunchtime hoping to find salvageable items. I left work early in the evenings to dig through the snow and debris. I rarely found anything, but I always held out hope. I awoke in the middle of one night with an idea. It could have been a dream. Possibly it was an answer to prayer.

Somehow, I knew the cloisonné vases and ivory carving of the Mother Mary were still on the hearth of the fireplace. Pat and I had purchased them in China in 1987 before we were married. We bought a set of two vases and each took one, with the idea that they might one day be reunited if we were to marry. And they were. We were married in 1991. I was assured in my dream they had survived the fire. It would be a miracle if this were accurate because the chimney and all that had remained of the house had been leveled and knocked into the basement with that major piece of equipment.

The sun was bright the next day when I made my noon visit to our property. I walked directly to the side of the house where I had the best view of the hearth. I could not believe my eyes. There stood the carved Mother Mary ivory statue sticking out of the snow with her hands in prayer. I wiped my eyes to be sure. The statue had been encased in Plexiglas, which must have saved it as the heat generated from the flames rose. The case was destroyed. I could not get to the statue. It was isolated on the fireplace hearth. The floor once beneath it was gone.

I called my son Scott and asked him to drive over and lay a ladder over the remaining beams to the hearth. He climbed out and retrieved the statue. When he handed it to me I saw minor scorching on the back, but the ivory was intact. And then, Scott found the cloisonné vases. I had been overwhelmed with grief by the loss of my family history held by the lost heirlooms, and especially for the loss of the fireman's life. But the reappearance of the ivory statue and those vases gave me solace and will always be treasured by me. There were no more items recovered after that discovery. I guess some dreams do come true.

# CHAPTER 30:

## *Moving Forward by Looking Back*

Joel C. Taylor & Esther Jane Woodin married 1863

The loss of the fireman's life and the mental recovery from the fire was rough for Pat and me but dealing with tragedy was nothing new for my family. My great-parents, Joel and Esther Jane Taylor each arrived in Grass Lake to buy land and farm during the Civil War. They lost three of their four children to tuberculosis, a deadly disease of that time. The pregnant Esther Jane Taylor was left with two children and a farm to run when her husband lost his life in a freak accident. I found his obituary in a stack of newspaper clippings in an old trunk at the farmhouse.

*Jackson Citizen*, May 30, 1876:
By special dispatch from Grass Lake we learn that Mr. Joel Taylor, an old resident of Grass Lake, while standing in front of his house Monday forenoon about 11 o'clock, during the storm that passed eastward about that time, was struck by lightning and instantly killed. Members of his family were standing around him at the same time, and some of them were badly shocked, but not seriously injured.

*Jackson Citizen*, June 6, 1876:
The funeral services of the late Joel Taylor were largely attended at the Baptist church on Wednesday at two o'clock. We learn but few more facts concerning his death. It seems he held a knife in his

hand with which he was cutting a whip for his little boy, and the theory is that the knife drew the death flash from the building that was struck first. Mr. Taylor leaves a wife and two children. He was widely known in this part of the county. With the exception of the hired girl, who was knocked down, the other members of the family, though quite near, were uninjured.

Esther Jane's diary May 29, 1876:
"Joel Taylor died at ½ past eleven and I and my children are in great sorrow". The next day she entered: "We are here with our neighbors in the greatest sorrow hearts can know; health very poor". On Sunday, just a few days later: "Stayed at home. A long, long day. Know not what can support me but the grace of God."

Amidst extreme sorrow following my great grandfather's death his wife, Esther Jane, survived the crisis by carrying on family traditions. She continued with her own chores and took care of her children while successfully managing the multiple-property farm. She did this until her death in 1902 at 62.

On January 29, 1877, seven months after her husband died, my great grandmother gave birth to her fourth child, Joel Clay.

Homestead circa 1864

# CHAPTER 31:

*Turning Tragedy Into Opportunity*

Anxiety filled both of our days for months. Eventually we came to realize that since we could not change what had happened we might as well focus our thoughts on being thankful for the fun times we had in our home before the fire. We were both determined to have a positive and satisfying future together. I continued work and so did Pat.

Our yearly skiing trip to Park City, Utah was on our calendars for a month after the disaster. Pat and I thought about canceling the trip but concluded it would be good to get away. Both of us needed a break from all the daily discussions and reminders of the tragedy. We met up with a group of friends from California at the ski resort who did not know about the fire, nor did we tell them until the following year. We were up and out early every morning, skied all day, and enjoyed drinks and dinner before going to bed each night. Physically exhausted, we could finally sleep. The exercise coupled with a new environment provided a perfect setting for our mental recovery.

Since we lost everything in the fire we decided to shop for clothes instead of skiing one day. Park City stores were about to get lucky. My usual way to shop when I spin off from Pat is to ask for a personal shopper. I go to buy, not shop. Pat has her own strategies that work for her. Each of us had our favored stores ship several boxes of new clothing back to Michigan.

Our future housing plans were decisions that required considerable thought and plenty of patience. We discussed the pros and cons of building a smaller home now that our children were all out on their own.

An older, smaller house sat on a beautiful lot adjacent to us. It faced the lake and was for sale. The property had a charming history and appeared to be a setting for good health and a long marriage. The same couple had owned it for 60 years. Both had recently passed away after more than 75 years of marriage.

We considered buying the lot, a more appropriate size for a smaller home, bulldozing the existing house and then building our own. Twelve houses had been developed on the north side of Brown's Lake around 1950 with a low turnover rate over the next 60 years. Nine had only been sold twice and three had been passed down to the next generation. We wanted to stay on the stable north side of the lake.

We considered the smaller home over the next two weeks, but my thinking began to change as I realized a small home would ruin the long-term value of the property. After all, Pat and I are long-term planners and thinkers. I came home one evening around the first of April to our rented home and said to my wife, "I think we should build a larger home, so we do not destroy the value of the property."

How long do you think it took Pat to answer? In a matter of a few seconds, she said, "I agree; let's start making plans." In that moment, we both knew we had shifted our thinking and feelings from a depressed mode to an attitude of promise and opportunity.

We drafted plans on plain paper for a two-story home, Pat on her drawing board and me on mine. We put them together and found no significant differences. I brought home graph paper the next day and we placed the rooms and layout to scale as best we could. The following day, we scheduled a meeting with Mike McKay, the premier builder of quality homes in the region.

While we waited at Mike's office to see him, I found an Anderson Window ad in a magazine for a northern-Michigan-type home with a high-peaked roof held up by solid oak beams. The upper level was two stories high with several windows across the front. The exterior colors were grey and blue, hues that complemented the fieldstone trim and pillars. I showed the picture to Pat. She said "yes." Then she found some great interior pictures in another magazine with a large, high fireplace that was the main focus in the great room. It had that wow factor we were looking for each time we walked into our new house. We showed our hand-drawn plans to Mike and he promised to get detailed professional drawings for us within ten days.

In the meantime, we were trying to settle the value of our fire-destroyed structure with Auto Owners Insurance. The contents settlement would come much later. The company argued we could save the foundation and build on it. McKay argued he would not build on the old foundation because of its age and heat damage. Auto Owners agreed with him in the end. Then the company selected another builder for a competitive bid on replacement cost. When the builder found out he would not get the contract, he had to be pushed to get his numbers in even though he was being paid to make the proposal.

Pat and I went through three sets of detailed plans over a three-week period before settling on one. A condition Pat and I included in the contract with McKay was that we are in our new home by that Christmas. He agreed to an accelerated schedule and gave us a price for a 5,000-square-foot home. We signed the contract and the project was on the fast track. Just think about it. We started with pieces of plain and graph paper and had the final plans in three weeks. When the home was finished there were only a couple of minor things we would have done differently. The key to Mike's meeting our move-in date was that we made quick decisions and did not change our minds. I have used the practice of making decisions quickly and changing my mind slowly to be effective in life and in business.

The insurance company made us a lowball offer on replacement cost for construction. It was clear they hoped we would settle quickly so they could write a check and move on. I have been involved in enough negotiations to know that we needed to be patient and not accept their first offer. Our builder helped by making major corrections to the insurance adjuster. Mike convinced their expert to agree with his numbers on replacement costs, which reconfirmed what I had learned about being patient and working with professionals.

Determining the amount of the personal property insurance claim with Auto Owners was another challenge. We interviewed a couple of insurance adjuster companies that wanted 10% of the personal property settlement as their fee. They would list all personal items in the house, the closets, cupboards, and dressers. We would help them arrive at the cost by considering when we had purchased the items. Then they would arrive at the replacement cost. This would be a long, tedious process and could take weeks. We discussed the condition of the site with the adjustors. Since almost everything had burned, Pat and I determined the two of us would do the best job listing what was not there, instead of working with a third party.

During one of my salvage missions, I remembered there was a small closet in the basement that held our collection of family photos tightly packed in wooden boxes. The boxes were surrounded on two sides by concrete walls. I had moved aside the burned door and could see the remnants of wooden boxes. I learned in my early days of accounting that client paper files could withstand a tremendous amount of fire and heat if they were tightly packed. I knew photo developers stacked photos together tightly for storage. I got lucky. I was able to rescue and sort three boxes of slightly burned envelopes and somewhat charred photos from the ashes. Even though I had transferred them to a new box, they still had a stench from the fire and smoke. I walked into our temporary home carrying the box. Pat got one whiff before asking, "What are you bringing home tonight?"

I worked every night for two months going through the photographs looking for a complete view of the contents of the inside of the house that were not in closets or drawers. I scoured clean a few personal items, including a partial set of antique dishes that were family hand-me-downs. I regret not taking indoor photos of our home, our closets and our drawers that could provide an inventory if needed in the future in case of fire or theft.

We began building our list of lost items room by room. We added to the list for the next 15 months. The insurance company required an estimated cost and replacement value for each item, proving our estimates of replacement cost if we did not actually buy the items. Auto Owners reimbursed us 100% of the replacement cost if we purchased and 70% if we did not. The list took at least 50 pages. Six years later, we still think of items left off the list. We'll be looking for a particular item and then suddenly realize, "Oh, it was lost in the fire."

I began to realize that my family's antiques were sentimental pieces, priceless to me, did not have much monetary value. Pat worked on the list almost every day. We both finally burned out on the project even though the adjuster said we still had some money left to claim. Pat and I agreed in the end that Auto Owners was a good and fair company.

Pat and I discussed a smaller 4-burner residential kitchen stove available from a local retailer, but then she changed her mind. She wanted two ovens. I asked her, "Will you cook two meals a week if you buy two ovens?" She said "yes," and we moved on. I visited the home during construction one day and there sat a commercial six-burner stove. I asked why we had to have a commercial stove and she replied that the other was proportionately too small to fit under the large exhaust fan cover. What can I say? I will say that she is a wonderful cook, and I have truly benefitted from our well-appointed kitchen.

The weeks counted down as we neared early December. We told Mike and the subcontractors that we had hired movers and would be moving in December 20. Mike told the subs we were not kidding, and they'd better be finished with their work. The day before the move eight people were still working on the project, including painters, wallpaper hangers, and decorators. We arrived on December 20 and all the interior workers were gone, although a few exterior workers were still on the site. Mike told us this was the first-time residents had moved into one of his homes while his crews were still working on the exterior. That was fine with us. The inside was certainly beautiful.

# CHAPTER 32:

## Preparation For Boating is Like Preparation in Life

Back in Florida we left Lake Okeechobee the next morning on *TransAction*. The Mercers were aboard. Our destination was the South Seas Plantation south of Fort Myers on the Gulf of Mexico. Along the way we cruised through beautiful green marshes with an abundance of wildlife. We especially enjoyed the low boat traffic.

Preparation is a big part of boating, just like it is in all business. I planned the next few days' destinations to keep us on target for our circle trip from the Gulf back to Miami. I spent time each evening carefully checking the charts and planning the navigation for tomorrow's voyage. Some days have much more adventure than others no matter how much planning I do.

We motored under the bridges on the Caloosahatchee River as we approached the Gulf and cautiously navigated into the plantation's harbor, which we learned had changed its name to the South Seas Island Resort. We refueled and headed to our boat slip. There was no saloon. There was no ash to clean from the white deck on the boat. Instead, golf courses, shops, and elegant restaurants surrounded the marina.

I recalled what Robert Fulgham said about the importance of learning some, thinking some and playing some. It was all about living a balanced life.

Since the days are short during the first half of January, we prepared to embark at sunrise. We especially wanted to take full advantage of daylight while we are navigating unknown waters. As the Mercers departed for the airport to return to the working world, we headed west out of the inland waterway into the Gulf of Mexico.

Our course would take us south to Marathon in the Florida Keys where we would reach deep water in the Gulf. I planned to take a direct course to keep us off the shallow waters 30 miles out from Naples and Marco Island. Cruising along at 20 knots, 23 mph, it was a perfect day. Pat was reading a book. I was focused on the gauges and surrounding waters. I glanced to the stern and was surprised to see we were churning mud. We were leaving a murky trail behind us and were 30 miles from land. How would I solve this challenge?

That is why we love boating. Every day offers new adventures. I feel the same way about starting a new business or meeting a new client. I would never have guessed my next business adventure would be a phone book.

I had been in unknown waters before. Instead of churning mud, this time we churned cash.

# CHAPTER 33:

## *New Industry: Unique Challenges*

Universal Publishing, Inc., or UPI, came to my attention in 1988 as a start-up company in need of investors. The owner, I'll call him Mr. Phone Book, had started the company with his wife and mother. All had experience producing and publishing a yellow-page phone book. I was impressed with their knowledge and talent in this industry. Mr. Phone Book had the ability to sell anything to anyone. He sold advertising for the UPI book, and eventually sold me on this venture.

UPI had access to the original telephone number listings from AT&T after a Supreme Court ruled that phone listings were public information and not owned by the phone companies. Each year UPI purchased the additions and deletions from AT&T to update their records. The price was fair, but as you can imagine after AT&T had enjoyed a monopoly in the phone book arena, they were not enthusiastic about providing information to a new competitor. They were slow delivering listings and did what they could to inconvenience competition. UPI hired experts to add new phone number listings and delete the old.

I invited two of my friends to participate in this venture. Addison P. Cook III was a natural fit. He grew up in Central Advertising Company, or CAC, an outdoor billboard advertising business. He had been a client since 1967. We had respect and trust in each other having participated in small investments since our initial meeting. Mr. Cook had capital and liked to work with young and upcoming entrepreneurs.

My goal was to have a team of associates in place before we negotiated an investment interest with UPI's current owner. I looked next to a successful attorney friend, Philip Curtis of the Curtis & Curtis PC law firm, to provide us with legal advice and capital, and to be a part of the management team. We had worked professionally with several mutual clients. People in the community frequently confused us for one another. It was not uncommon for people to call me Curtis and him Willis.

Conversations with Mr. Phone Book continued day and night. We spent hours learning the business. The UPI phone book for Jackson and the surrounding areas was much more comprehensive and covered a larger area than the AT&T utility book. We understood that all the money Mr. Phone Book had collected on the presale of ads had already been spent accumulating and assembling the massive data needed to publish the book. He needed capital to print and deliver the book. Our investment group analyzed strategies and budgets and formulated an agreeable plan to invest in UPI.

We presented the investment plan, and after negotiation and some compromises had an agreement. The three new investors would provide capital and operational input as minority owners. The current owner would have voting rights and management control. Investors commonly take control of the voting shares of a company. Debt financing with conversion options for stock ownership is a common investment structure when the assets of the company are secured as collateral for the loan. Operators who have a majority ownership are motivated to be successful. Their success will, in turn, result in success for the investors.

I tried to do my share after closing the investment. Normally with a startup my contribution would be contributing ideas to help save money, create efficiencies, or increase sales. I might recommend and implement savings ideas for reducing state or federal income taxes, property taxes, or insurance costs. Or, I might assist in creating a favorable bank loan package to reduce interest fees or to provide additional capital for business growth.

With UPI we became involved in all phases of the business. The investment team scheduled weekly meetings to set goals and keep the team focused and working on daily operating improvements. I provided a written agenda.

These forums were often where new ideas were generated. We challenged management on future plans. We set timeframes for each company goal and assigned responsibilities. The regular meetings provided a format for the follow-up and the monitoring process. I assigned someone on the team to be a note taker.

My first assistant at my accounting firm, Ina Rombyer, gave me an interesting Christmas present one year. It was a small bedside clipboard with a notepad, flashlight, and attached pencil. She knew I would get up in the middle of the night to jot down things to do and ideas for my own business or ideas for clients. She knew because I arrived at the office each morning loaded for bear. Her gift was a tool to capture ideas and lock them in for future reference.

Everyone has the capacity to come up with ideas that will enhance the lives of their family, business, or community, but successful people continue learning, gain experiences and store their ideas in a deep brain database. When it's appropriate they implement those ideas. I tend to read autobiographies of successful people and use what they said they learned to help develop my life and career.

Our core team at UPI probed to learn more about the key drivers of the yellow-book industry, and then set the goals that would provide our long-term success.

Mr. Phone Book was a typical visionary entrepreneur. His smile would beam, and his mind was overflowing with ideas on how to make UPI the biggest and best in his industry. He wanted to produce a book that would make the competition envy our product, a book that would drive the customers to our new and larger advertisers. He was well informed and correct in determining the driver for future revenue was user-demand. And he had ways of determining customer usage.

One idea was to reduce the price as an incentive for a customer to place an ad in our book. A new telephone number was listed in the ad to track phone calls. AT&T records verified the number of calls. The units were astounding, exceeding the expectations of the advertisers by thousands of calls. In turn, these advertisers became ready buyers for the next year's book.

Our team of investors knew nothing about the yellow page industry at the time, but we did understand the process before we invested our money. Of course, the goal of any business investment is to earn a profit, but primarily we wanted to provide new jobs in the Jackson area. The exit plan for our investment was to sell to the company's founder or to another entity.

Jackson's phone book was ready to publish. Now it needed to be printed and delivered. The commitment to deliver 75,000-plus books in Jackson and adjoining counties was astronomical.

Our visionary leader had surpassed his goals when it came to printing and delivering the book. The book was filled with so much information that it took more pages than anticipated and went over budget. It took more paper, more freight, more set-ups, and more delivery costs. I recall that the overrun costs were about a third more than our initial budget of $300,000, a surprise to investors and then a disappointment. A shortage of capital would have immediately ended the project, and someone else would have taken over the market area for pennies on our dollar. We were prepared and invested more capital.

Our team had questions. We knew we had to raise our revenue projections for the future, but could it be done? Would customers shift to our independent book from the well-established book? Would UPI still be around next year if the books were delivered six months late? Could we produce and pay for the next books? Would customers give us deposits on next year's books or be concerned because we changed our timeline? Could we be successful, financially, in this industry? We immediately accelerated the team meetings.

I base decisions on long-term thinking. Short-term decisions almost always cost more money and reduce long-term rewards.

We developed good accounting systems for UPI. We investors did not deposit the receipts or write the checks but established good internal accounting controls to see that the money was handled accurately and properly. While analyzing the financial data and preparing projections for the next book, we needed to move quickly since the selling process for the next edition started immediately following the delivery of the previous book. In the meantime, we were receiving good feedback.

Visionary entrepreneurs frequently have no fear of failure and look only at the upside. These folks are exciting to be around. Failure is not an option. The four-minute mile is a good example. Prior to May 6, 1954, it was thought that humans were incapable of running a mile in less than four minutes, an idea that was accepted as fact. Englishman Rodger Bannister proved it could be done. Once he officially broke the world record, it was broken repeatedly. In the past 50 years the time has been cut by 17 seconds.

Visionaries believe they can be successful. While some see all the cautions and pitfalls and never even try, others jump in and go for it. Successful inventors often start with a dream to resolve a problem and refuse to take no for an answer.

> Give me the courage, Lord, to sail
> my boat out from the shore.
> I'd rather know the oceans gale
> and hear the tempests roar
> than anchor safely in some bay
> because fear conquered me.
> Let craft less daring inland stay...
> be mine the pathless sea.
> Joseph Morris

One day Mr. Phone Book called so full of excitement he could barely speak. Three failed books in other Michigan cities were for sale. He was hyperventilating and said we had to get our offer to purchase the books in fast or other buyers would scoop them up. I suggested he take a deep breath.

I was still trying to comprehend how he could possibly be dreaming of other markets when we had our hands full in Jackson. He pointed out the benefits of having four markets and developing two sales teams that would rotate between the four markets. We would utilize sales people year around, which, he felt, would allow us to attract higher quality people.

He had financial information on the other books, including population, number of books needed, ads sold, and market potential. I was trying to calculate the cost versus the value and benefits. We investors were in the dark on the potential. We still had not yet completed a year cycle of the Jackson book.

Mr. Phone Book and I continued to gather information and prepare for a presentation after we scheduled a meeting of investors. He estimated it would take $1,000,000 to buy the books and move into the expanded market. The actuality of it was that the purchase price was zero, but we had to agree to assume the liability of publishing and delivering the books. We would receive the existing accounts receivable and assume the accounts payable. The existing markets would be ours, but they were by no means exclusive ownership. Anyone else could enter the market and compete with AT&T and us. Were there other giants in the industry with a team and deep pockets that could enter these markets and bury us in the process? Was a million dollars enough to satisfy the liabilities we would assume? We were excited about the potential.

The discussion had continued for two and a half hours when we decided to make an offer for Ann Arbor and Lansing. The consensus was that the Saginaw market lacked potential. I left the meeting assuming the remaining three would make an offer on two markets.

I woke up the next morning wondering what took place. I had several other items on my agenda and expected that one of our three principals would contact me. I did not hear a word, so late that evening I called Mr. Phone Book. "How did it go? What happened?" I assumed nothing as no one had contacted me. He was still hyperventilating and finally stated: "We purchased all three markets." I asked him to repeat his statement. "We purchased all three markets. We take over tomorrow!" I could not possibly comprehend what we were in for in the future. To be honest, none of us had a clue. We were following the dream of a visionary entrepreneur.

The process began by our assuming liabilities, finding enough office space, building an expanded management team, and transferring sales staff from the prior company. Mr. Phone Book could make large jobs seem simple. That was largely because he could only see the destination and not all the roads it would take to get there.

We investors had built organizations before but none the size of this project. We were about to add jobs in Jackson, which was great. The first hire was my son Phil who was on break from Jackson Community College. Mr. Phone Book said we needed someone for a couple of weeks to copy records, build files, and transfer data from the seller. Ten years later, Phil was still there.

We did not have enough room in the small office on Jackson's Ganson Street and moved to a building purchased by Mr. Cook. The activity was fast and furious. We had assumed all the responsibilities of the acquisitions and simultaneously were trying to run a sales campaign for Jackson.

We were now in business across Michigan, plus we had regional and national advertising. So, we knew we needed to upgrade our accounting and internal control system. We initially hired a part-time, semi-retired accountant, Ernie Bako. We outgrew his capacity and added Judy McCaslin. We advertised locally for a full-time controller and hired Morris Conklin. After Morris, we expanded by adding Carolyn McIvor. We now had an extremely talented and dedicated team.

Things were flying fast as we built our sales team and blended them with the sales staff we acquired in the purchase. We eventually hired a sales manager. Things were firing on all cylinders; excitement and morale were high. Implementing a yellow page ad design center, my son Phil accepted employment in that department. Under the direction of veteran Mary Hall, this team won several national awards for yellow page design.

The Jackson book closed with the completion of the campaign. Then, a surprise. Because of expanded content it was 50% over budget. We investors added additional capital to cover expenses. Mr. Phone Book was an extremely creative person, but rarely considered the cost of his designs and product enhancements.

We began to extrapolate the costs of the books in the new markets and realized we needed to be creative in generating more revenue in all the markets. How do we obtain new customers and ad renewals in cities where the previous product was good but delivered six months late? There were ongoing brainstorming sessions on pricing structure, incentives, and discounts for early payments to generate cash flow. The sales commission structure was complicated, but the design was to generate more revenue from existing customers, add new customers, and encourage up-front cash payments.

The new Jackson book was more complicated than the prior year and delivery would be delayed at least a month. The month delay cost us 1/12 of the annual revenue because each book needed a 12-month shelf life. Wow, this was a complex business. We attempted to look on the positive side of things. The Jackson book did show significant sales growth even though it missed our goal. The book was also generating support in our local community where we knew many of our advertisers.

Once again, the investors added more capital. We could not add enough capital on a pro rata basis, and realized we needed to borrow money. Bankers were unwilling to loan us money because we were a start-up business with no prior track record and had yet to show a profit on any of the books. A. P. Cook stepped up and pledged some of his investment securities to gain a loan. UPI paid him a loan guarantee fee to reward him for his additional risk. The loans, of course, began to add additional expense.

The sales campaigns ended in Ann Arbor and Lansing. Consistent with the Jackson book, the sales increase was offset with higher expenses.

Finding and training sales people in the yellow page business is as complicated as the development of any sales team. Since there is considerable "cold calling" involved, it is difficult to find people successful at this technique. In addition, we had to overcome the late delivery of the first book and leery, unwilling customers who wondered if UPI would survive. The delivery date of the second round of books was also deferred a month for numerous reasons. The cost of publishing, printing, and delivery of the new books continued to increase. The delay of a month again cost us another 30 days of lost revenue.

Regular meetings were held with the investors and Mr. Phone Book, who continued his enthusiasm and positive attitude. At this point he had no money to invest, so he had everything to gain and nothing to lose. With him continuing to paint a rosy picture, we three investors, being entrepreneurs, agreed to keep moving forward.

Our future meetings focused on building a better sales team, redesigning the books to reduce costs, and creating a tighter schedule for on-time delivery. Every one of these challenges, or opportunities, was going to take a great deal of management planning. We advertised heavily looking for more sales people and continued to build the team. We put out quotes for printing and saved costs with a new printer. On-time delivery was no longer a goal. It was a necessity.

Only a tight core of people realized our financial problems. We did not want our team at-large to know. We wanted them working with comfort and confidence that we were going to be successful. There was always money in the checkbook to make payroll, pay taxes, and pay the vendors' invoices, although the money was frequently wired in the day it was needed.

We were beginning the second round of the three new books armed with a new budget, more employees, and plenty of confidence. Our budget projected losses on all three books and a break-even on the Jackson book...plus an additional large investment of capital.

Sales for those campaigns improved over the first year but were again short of budget. The expenses came in over budget but also had improved over the prior year's numbers. The questions persisted: Could we compete? Could we ever make money in this industry? Would someone else enter the independent market as a competitor? Another independent in the market would have ruined the chance for any of us to being successful against AT&T. There were rumors of others entering the market and we had to stake our markets to look strong to any prospective competitors.

Managing UPI was like attaining any goal. You fix one thing by plugging the hole and something else breaks.

It's continual improvement. We were never satisfied even though it was working. We always asked how we could make it better, faster, or improve the infrastructure.

# CHAPTER 34:

## *Staying the Course*

UPI joined the national organization of independent yellow page book companies. The industry was growing, and we were beginning to see success stories around the country. We attended seminars at our first quarterly meeting and were able to see first-hand how other companies operated. We cemented friendships with other owners, shared names of suppliers and worked together on common interests and goals. This gave us more enthusiasm to push forward.

I attended one meeting in North Dakota with my son, Phil. We planned extra time at the top of the trip to do some touring of local interest in the area. We visited Fort Custer where the General made his last stand. The meeting schedule included morning meetings, a noon social, and a networking dinner. I found the social time most beneficial because I could discuss subjects that directly impacted our own company and circumstances.

The North Dakota host company was one of the first in the industry and had a wide market area because of the sparse population. The business was capital intensive and money was difficult to find, so the owners took the company public to raise capital. I spoke to the owners about the capital they raised and asked questions. Speaking in confidence they told me they regretted taking their company public. The owner told me they were too small and were overburdened with costs and the scrutiny that goes with a public company. That discussion discouraged me from further consideration of taking UPI public.

I attended another meeting in Hawaii. This time Pat joined me. The conference was well organized and attended by independents from all over the U.S. It was at a snazzy hotel on a Maui beach. From our room, we watched the humpback whales cruise the ocean. When the sessions began, I attended every one and asked question after question. I gathered business cards to build a database of contacts to provide future answers I may need in a short period of time. This business, like every business, was about whom you know versus what you know.

I realized early in my career how important it is to be able to rely on the judgment and input of other people and began building a database of people and professionals from all walks of life. When I need additional knowledge, this tool is at my fingertips.

The first directory I used was a reference index tool for names, addresses, and phone numbers. It had a sliding selector on one side using alpha tabs to quickly access a person's contact information. I inherited it by luck from a departing employee at my previous job and began gathering names and phone numbers of almost everyone I met. The index had great capacity and my resource list grew. 50 years later I will use it.

The world and I evolved the first time with the introduction of the Blackberry. Contacts from my manual system converted easily to the expanded capability of the Blackberry. I collected business cards at every opportunity and entered the data into my phone. The world and I evolved a second time with the introduction and expanded capability of the iPhone. I now have over 2000 contacts.

I often sit in meetings where members would love to get information on how to get something done right away. I say, "Do you want me to call them on their cell, now?" I refer to my database, make the call, and keep making calls until I get the particulars we need. Most people appreciate my calling to ask for their advice. They see that I respect them and their expertise. My fingertip database allows me to multi-task and enhances my productivity exponentially. Two heads are better than one.

I grew up a bashful farm kid from Grass Lake protected in my years preceding college. I accepted what I was told, trusting my family and the wisdom of people in our farming community. Questions were rarely posed. My coming of age and questioning everything started later.

I have learned over the years that people respect and are generally pleased to answer questions or assist in personal or business matters. It always helps to start your question with something like: "I was impressed when speaking with you," or, "I understand you are the expert about xyz." Most people cannot wait for the question or area of expertise where they can lend a helping hand. Today you can evaluate their advice and continue with your research on the internet.

We set the highest ethics and moral character standards for our employees and ourselves. We made promises to our customers and suppliers, and we carried them out. There would be no apologies for non-performance. We would exceed expectations.

Our employees had to be loyal and motivated and, perhaps most importantly, they needed to maintain a positive attitude. There was no room for negative thinkers. Non-believers would not survive in UPI. Most people fit right in and realized it was a team effort. Everyone had to carry his or her own load. It took all the team working and thinking every day on ways to improve their performance to make this company successful. We built a great core of people who followed those beliefs.

Mr. Phone Book decided in the third year that we should add color to our advertisements. "Wow," I thought. "It's a great idea but no one in the country was doing four-color ads in the yellow page book industry. I asked what the additional cost would be. Our visionary always responded with a huge smile and replied, "Not much."

Well, by then I knew not much meant more money. I appreciated his vision for setting us apart from the rest of the industry but challenged him on whether this innovation was achievable. I had doubts about the quality of four-color ads. He said we could charge our clients more money for the ads to cover our expenses with the understanding that their ads would get more attention than their former black on yellow ads.

We investors approved his proposal and proceeded with year four of the Jackson book. Many on staff doubted the new concept would take off. Our sales staff surprised us and sold a significant number of color ads at the increased price. The Jackson market was beginning to buy into our product, which was by then significantly better than our competition.

My son Phil was the design artist at the time. He developed ads with guidance from Mr. Phone Book and Mary Hall. The sales people were also contributing creative ideas for their customers. Our whole team was pulling together to see who could get the best ad.

We did not understand how successful the color ads were until the annual meeting in Las Vegas of the Independent Phone Books Association. We had entered our ads in several classifications of competition. The awards typically went to larger companies that started in business before us and were backed by large corporations. We were pleasantly shocked when we won the APPY Award for the best ad of the year, an ad designed by my son Phil featuring the bright colors of Spiderman.

UPI was little known before this meeting except for the one-on-one encounters we had at prior meetings. The national organization now recognized us as one of the most creative, leading-edge companies in the country. When we brought our trophy home we were welcomed to Jackson by a staff of believers. This award was a major turning point for UPI. Our success looked promising.

Our Jackson book was profitable in the fourth year. We pushed to improve operations every day. The owners were beginning to believe we would get a return on investment, or ROI, at some point down the road. We investors took a small compensation preferring to reinvest in the business. These sacrifices in the early years helped us preserve working capital and permitted us to continue building the business.

I have observed that too many businesses fail in the early years because the owners believe the business owes them a nice salary and lots of benefits. Often, the first thing tradesmen do when they start a new business is purchase a big fancy truck, sometimes before they even have customers. Then they finance the business by requiring big customer deposits before they start a job, saying the deposit is to buy materials. Then they charge the materials and spend the money on necessities and personal luxuries.

Next, they must find a new customer to get a deposit and pay for the materials of the last job. Before they know it, they are in a rat race, chasing new sales and deposits to secure their jobs, and running to their suppliers to pay bills so they can buy materials for the current job. They spend half their time chasing money rather than doing productive work. Their business would have been significantly more profitable had they started with some capital and an old truck and preserved the early profits to build healthy cash balances.

I insist on following the practice of conservative fiscal management in all companies in which I invest. We do not waste time or effort in money-chasing exercises. We pay bills on time and take full advantage of any discounts offered. I find that adequate capital provides buying power and opens doors to new opportunities. Buying power reduces costs and improves gross profit margins, improving a company's competitive edge, which in turn improves the bottom-line.

I have always followed the management policy of leading by example. It's essential that management set high ethical standards for all to follow. If I want my employees to start work at eight, I better be there before they were. If I want my staff to follow and make ethical decisions, I better do the same.

Unfortunately, in UPI, issues came to light that made it evident that we had some major differences in management style. We needed to make changes in leadership, and it would not be an easy decision to make. Investors and other key members of the operating team concluded that we would buy out Mr. Phone Book's share of stock.

Whenever a major player exits a company, the necessary changes can take their toll on employees. That was truly the case at UPI. We needed to rebuild confidence and establish our moral character and leadership. Restoring confidence was our number one issue to keep our team together and productive.

The investors delivered the news to staff personally. We spent more time with all departments in the company and made trips to the other offices thanking them for their efforts. Many were relieved by the changes we made, but there were many unanswered, burning questions about the future. We set new expectations and goals for the employees, monitored their progress and rewarded them along the way.

Unlike AT&T, we invoiced customers separate from the phone bills. We implemented strict policies and procedures for accepting new ad contracts and receivable collections. It took a couple of full-time employees in our collections department to manage the thousands of accounts. We structured the business, so the collections department approved the sales.

Of course, the sales department wanted sales, but oftentimes the client had an outstanding balance. In that instance the salesperson had to return with money to complete their contract. We restructured contracts so that corporations and LLC's had to have a personal guarantor as well. We maintained the process of daily improvement, separating the receivables and cash handling for better internal controls. Morris Conklin was the controller and Judy McCaslin was our accountant.

We began advertising for applicants for a chief operating officer, or COO. This person would work directly with the stockholders, carry out their assignments, and build morale. We hired a promising professional who had worked with the local hospital and supervised 700 volunteers. We had about 70 employees at the time. She looked like a natural fit with a great smile and positive personality.

We still had our work cut out for our team and for us. We started the fourth round of the acquired books. We had lost money on each of them for the first three years, although Lansing and Ann Arbor were showing some promise. The Jackson book was making money and looking better each year. We were the book of choice in the Jackson market. Sales in Jackson exceeded our other cities, that had much larger populations. It crossed our minds that it would have been easier to have stopped with the original book. There are always second thoughts in business.

Our new COO was busy fine-tuning our policies and implementing new ideas. She planned trips for the families and employees. We were all energized!

UPI Spine

# CHAPTER 35:

## *Insubordination*

We had an important choice to make on a new software system that was used to produce our books. The system managed the flow of the ads and white page listings for production, important customers, and accounting information. We found a couple of companies that provided potential systems. Investors held meetings with the team selected to make the decision and decided on the process. The plan was to select the best software following an on-site investigation of the program in operation.

One supplier for the new software was in Florida. My son Phil was software savvy and was not pleased with the product of this company. He voiced his opposition at the team meeting. I told our team we would make the decision in a month following my on-site visitation, and the weekly meetings continued with the software discussion put on hold.

When I arrived at the yellow page publication in Orlando, they welcomed me and made an informal presentation of the new software. I noticed limited use of important processes. They responded that the processes were not functioning or that they did not have instructions on how to use it. The decision was clear in my mind. We will not purchase this software.

I returned from my Florida trip and presented my findings to the team. I told them we should not order the system because it had not been proven in the field. Unfortunately, our COO had decided to purchase the system without owner approval and had already started implementation.

I was upset and did more investigation on the software internally. I could see we were headed for disaster. Employees pointed out problems during implementations.

The software did not perform. We had to abort it when our production staff realized it was not going to work. The result was that the decision cost us $250,000. I was extremely upset. It was no surprise to me, which proves that team decisions are usually the best.

Shareholders voted to terminate our COO for insubordination. We discussed the possibility of promoting from within. When we realized we did not have anyone on staff with both people and business skills, we placed some ads and discussed our job opening with placement service companies to find more qualified persons. Two weeks later we reviewed prospects for CEO but had no strong candidates. Out of the blue we heard Mr. Cook say, "I'm going to be the CEO!"

He did have the authority to appoint himself as CEO because he owned more than 50% of UPI. Mr. Cook certainly had a vested interest. Much of his personal financial security was on the line, counting on the success of UPI. He was an excellent candidate, and he was only 60 years old at the time.

Addison P. Cook III had leadership experience acquired with his development of Central Advertising, and he had excellent people skills. We questioned him about his willingness to commit enough time to handle the job. It had been 15 years since he sold Central Advertising and retired. Was he willing to come out of retirement? Would he give up his winters in California with his wife, Beatrice? Could he share responsibilities with others?

We met again a week later to discuss our future. Mr. Cook had considered his decision in depth and had lengthy discussions with his wife. He entered the meeting enthused and committed to be the CEO. We all had a lot riding on the future success of UPI, and on Addison P. Cook III.

A new era began when A.P. was elected the new CEO of UPI. As owner-manager, he assumed the responsibility of managing the sales team. I managed the finances, Phil Curtis managed legal issues, and A.P. and I managed production.

UPI had a unique product but we all knew it was sales that would produce a positive bottom line. A.P. and Thad Russell worked on ideas to promote sales every day.

They had more sales promotions and rewards and bonus programs than you can imagine. Things were jumping at the sales meetings, which were now scheduled for early Monday mornings and Friday afternoons to keep the sales people engaged 40-plus hours per week.

It was our sixth year in business in 1995, and we had lost money every year. Our bank did not renew the loan, so we found a new bank. Most investors would have given up long before this, but not our team. We saw potential and kept the pedal to the metal working consistently day in and day out. We all knew that perseverance and constant improvement were the keys to long-term success. We kept the squeeze on expenses and watched as revenues kept growing.

That year we hit our growing sales goal. We kept up with new technologies, continued to invest in our people, and attended meetings of our association. We also decided to offer stock options to key people in the company based on their years of service and their perceived value to the company. They could purchase UPI stock in the future at the price it was valued at in 1995, giving them a vested interest in the company. This was our carrot, our way of keeping our key people motivated

The year 1996 brought about the need for additional capital. Mr. Cook said he was tapped out and I did not blame him for saying so. Our budgets and cash flow forecast showed we needed $250,000 to get through the year. I placed a second mortgage on my office building to raise funds for what we expected to be the final investment. We met our goals that year, and for the first time we did not lose money.

The year 1997 brought more growth in revenue. The business was now fun and exciting, and the morale of the employees was great. Mr. Cook provided extra spark to the sales force, giving them almost everything they asked for. They loved him, and his leadership was producing results.

The year was magical as we made a profit. We began to pay down debt. We took nominal compensation to improve the balance sheet and the capital structure. We saw our profit continue to grow in 1998 and made a seven-figure bottom line. The next year brought us even more good news.

TransWestern Publishing, a growing company based in California, approached us in mid-1999 to discuss a possible sale to them. We discussed it internally and decided we would talk to them. We had concerns about the risks of new technology and what would happen with the hard copy of the yellow page book.

I prepared a short version of what I thought would be a fair value for our stock. My numbers exceeded the anticipated value of the other two principal shareholders, and included a three-year projection of revenue, expenses, net income, and cash flow based on our historical growth.

The prospective buyers came to Jackson for the meeting. We knew they were qualified buyers, already running a good business, and were financially prepared to make a purchase. We held a two-hour lunch meeting. Both sides evaluated the other to determine who held the upper hand in the negotiations.

We told them we were concerned about the jobs for our people and that we would like the home base of operations to be in Jackson. We negotiated a provision that they would hire every employee even though they would be moving production to California. They agreed to offer every employee a job in the sales department for a year regardless of their sales skills and training.

We both signed confidentiality agreements. We provided them with the financial information they needed. The acquisition of Lansing, Ann Arbor, and Saginaw was now providing extra value due to the size of our market territory. They told us they would give us an offer the following week.

Their offer arrived on schedule and was close to my calculated value based on a multiple of 10 times the cash flow. We principals discussed the offer and accepted it subject to some modifications. This was an asset purchase, meaning they bought our assets and goodwill. They assumed no liabilities and we paid our debts.

Employees were surprised and disappointed when we made the announcement. They had become comfortable with the owner-managed style of operation where they felt part of the family. And they were part of our family. We pre-scheduled job training and job placement services for those who wanted them, or they could opt for unemployment benefits. My son Phil accepted the sales job, gained valuable experience and moved on to another job after the first year.

We owners were proud of the people and businesses we had worked with over the years. Our team at UPI shared that pride. We still hold annual reunion luncheons. UPI Management was satisfied we had achieved the goal of creating jobs in Jackson. We enjoyed a financially rewarding experience in return, at last. We extended employee payroll for a period after the sale and recognized our loyal team with a fully funded 401K-retirement plan for the year following the sale to TransWestern. The additional employee payments amounted to about $700,000.

TransWestern sold UPI to Yellow Book a few years later. They now dominate the U.S. yellow book industry with mostly online services.

Phil Curtis, A.P. Cook and Phil Willis

# CHAPTER 36:

## *A New Challenge*

Churning chaos back on *TransAction*, it was clear we had reached a shallow area thirty miles offshore. The sea was brown mud. I slowed the speed and placed the gears in neutral while I took a closer look at the charts. I checked our GPS location and determined we were too close to the mainland even though we were 30 miles offshore. Instead of continuing in unknown waters I decided to retrace our murky trail until we reached deep water. I made a large circle to the west and south. The maneuver was a success. As we began to cruise at full speed I wondered what the towboat pirate would have charged for service out here, three hours from nowhere.

At noon we entered the treacherous waters that lead to the Keys. Pat had prepared a beautiful lunch on deck. I placed the boat on autopilot to slowly maintain our course and to enjoy the scenery and meal. After lunch, Pat gave me a short break at the helm and we proceeded with care.

Now we were entering the dangerous area my sister Marilyn had warned us about, the area that included narrow, shallow waters laced with sand bars and reefs.

We slowed the engines to idle and entered the marked channels with caution. The next 25 miles required identifying every marker buoy starting with number one green on the port and number two red on the starboard. Pat alternately stood and sat on the bow looking for the buoys and casing the shallows. Some markers were missing. We were both attentive and maneuvered the buoys and sandbars to the Marathon area and marina without a glitch.

The next morning, we left Marathon under clear skies and light winds and arrived in Highland Beach mid-afternoon, right on schedule. We had completed our ten-day trip in nine. That extra day became a bonus. We spent it with my mother and then flew home to Michigan.

We had learned a lot these past few days, like we do every time we take our boat out. Our level of skills shifted after this trip, giving us more confidence and planting seeds for further adventures with friends and family.

# CHAPTER 37:

## Investing with Friends and Family

Some people say the best way to hurt relationships with family and friends is to go into business with them. I have found the opposite to be true, if the business venture is sound. Over the years I have implemented my process over and over with different investments in many industries.

A long-time family friend, Donald Dakin, called me in 1979 to discuss a business venture. He had been working as a mechanic at a garage service station and serviced Coca Cola delivery trucks on the side. He had an opportunity to buy a lawn and garden equipment retail and service business. The Scheele-Ludlow Lawn Equipment business, established in Jackson in 1955 by Mr. Ludlow, was one of the first stand-alone outdoor power equipment businesses in the country at a time when Michigan was a worldwide leader in manufacturing and a major center for the creation of many new inventions and ideas.

The business was closed in July that same year with an auction by order of the City Bank & Trust who held the credit line. Don's dream was to run his own business. He had contacted an investor about restarting the business but needed $40,000 for the buyout and some working capital. Don Dakin had the expertise to run the business but needed cash. He said he had another party willing to invest $20,000 if he could find the other $20,000.

The William Dakin family had lived in our farm tenant house, just 500 feet from our home. They operated our dairy farm at 2215 Willis Road in the early 1950s under the management of my dad, Phil Sterling Willis. I first remember Don as a three-year-old. I may have been about eight at the time. We would meet up in the farmyard and entertain each other playing with all the domestic animals and getting into trouble.

My brother Larry and I did have one responsibility on the farm at that time. Our summer job was to plant, weed, and harvest the bounty from a small garden patch south of the corncrib. Dad would have the garden plowed in the spring. I learned from that experience how to plant and bury seeds in a straight line by pounding stakes at each end of the garden and attaching a string between the stakes. After planting one row we would move the stakes over a foot or more, carefully aligning the rows. The only tools we had were a hoe and a three-prong hand cultivator that we pushed between the rows to eliminate some the weeds. It took both of us to push the cultivator; the handles were about head high for us. Oh, how we hated to pull weeds in the heat of the summer. Of course, we could have pulled weeds in the early morning when it was still cool, but we never got started until late afternoon just before Dad was scheduled to arrive home from work. I remember trying to bribe Donald Dakin into helping us pull weeds.

I thought over Don's investment opportunity for a couple of days. I wanted to get involved with my old friend and help him achieve his dream, so I scraped up the $20,000 from savings. I called Don and told him I was ready to start the due diligence process and asked to meet the other investor before proceeding with the private equity investment. It would be another step toward building my personal assets. I would be investing in our community plus I would be helping a friend.

Our entire company team had to be approved by the seller, the franchises and the manufacturers. This was a complicated process. Although the retailer sold Allis Chalmers equipment, the business was a retail lawn and garden vendor. They had added Cub Cadet equipment manufactured by International Harvester.

The other investor was Dale Gaide, DVM. Dale was and is a veterinarian specializing in large animals, primarily horses. At one time, he and his wife, Irene, had a farm north of Jackson with their own track where they bred and trained thoroughbreds.

Our meeting with Dale proved positive. Although Don Dakin told us the business had closed because of poor management and Don admitted he did not have a proven track record for running a business, we decided to go forward. Dale and I believed in Don Dakin. It was risky, but each of us invested $20,000 with the unproven businessman in a formerly failed business. We set up a new corporation with Dale and I each receiving 45% of the stock and Don receiving 10%.

Investing and private equity capital, more times than not, follow the "Golden Rule." In other words, those who have the gold, rule. Don Dakin had faith in Dale and me, and we, in him. He worked for us as president of the company. His management skills determined if we made or lost our money. Successful relationships are built by having faith and trust in your partners and "doing your share and a little bit more."

Don Dakin was a smart man. He knew enough at three years old not to toil in the sun with those garden weeds for the piddling sum I offered. We could see he was a great salesman. He treated us with respect as we did him. We continued meeting while Don negotiated the approval of the manufacturer and franchises. My standard condition when I invest in a company is that our firm be the accountant and prepare tax returns, so I can follow the financial end of the business. Both Don and Dale agreed since we needed an accountant.

The Donald Dakin family relationship turned out to be closer than we could have imagined. Don's dad was recruited away from our farm to be the lead mechanic at the Chelsea Implement Company in Chelsea, about 10 miles east of Grass Lake. Don's mother, Joan, raised the family and managed the household. The Chelsea Implement Company started by my Uncle Dean Willis in 1946, initially was supported by family investment.

During our conversations to organize the yard and garden we learned our families had more in common than we knew. My father had advertised for another family to operate the farm after the Dakins left. He hired the Millard Hashley family. They were the perfect farm family fit with eleven strong, healthy children. Mary Hashley was one of their children. When she grew up she married Don Dakin.

The Hashley family operated our farm at 2215 Willis Road for many years until Millard was recruited to work at my dad's business as the lead mechanic at the Grass Lake Implement Co. Farm hands had to be great mechanics to keep everything running. I was beginning to like this relationship with Don Dakin even more, knowing that we were dealing with the respected families of Dakin and Hashley.

We closed the deal on the new business, and on October 10, 1979, Yard-N-Garden Equipment, Inc. was registered with the State of Michigan. The day after Thanksgiving, Don opened for business. For the balance of the winter months, Don hired a part-time employee to work alongside him. At the beginning, growth was slow but Don's perseverance and hard work began to show results. He not only worked hard, he was also smart in his operations. He continued monthly meetings with the investors, welcoming our input. One day Dale came to the meeting and suggested the business name be changed to include Don's name. I thought that was a great idea; the business soon became known as Dakin's Yard & Garden Equipment, Inc. Customers liked doing business with an owner. They knew Don would be there to provide support and service when needed.

At the time, Carolyn and I were married. I had placed her name on the shares of stock to minimize estate taxes. When my dad died, my family had been burned by estate taxes, so I was extremely conscious of the demon federal estate tax. I was also in the profession that assisted in the design of family estate plans. Dividing assets was the way to go if your goal was to build your net worth.

Don's goal from the beginning was to own 100% of the stock in the company. A few years went by and, operating on an extremely conservative management policy, the company accumulated cash. The years moved on and the business continued to grow. Then, as happens in many marriages, Carolyn and I divorced, and she received our Yard and Garden Equipment, Inc. stock as part of the divorce settlement. Now I was providing accounting services for my ex-wife, which made me a little uncomfortable. The stock assignment to Carolyn turned out well for everyone. Carolyn's desire was to sell the stock and convert it to cash. Don purchased Carolyn's stock and then owned controlling interest in the company.

Don pursued Dale Gaide to sell his stock, so he would have a 100% ownership. We did not have a buy-sell agreement but had generally decided in the beginning that it was the investors' goal to help Don get started in business and earn a return on our investment. Dale eluded Don for some years since Dale enjoyed the relationship and some benefits he was receiving. Don finally pinned Dale down. He purchased the stock in 1995. The sale completed the transition from an investor-controlled company to a family owned business.

My personal relationship with the Dakin's grew over the years. Our children worked summers occasionally for each other's family gaining experience in the working world and in a different industry. The cross training did not produce future jobs, but the children gained valuable experience.

While still in school, John, Don and Mary's son, began working part-time for Dakin's Yard & Garden Equipment to learn the business. Following graduation, he came on board full-time. As a reward and incentive to stay with the business and produce like an owner, he was issued stock in the company. Don and Mary's other children, Kathy, Nancy, and Chris, helped at some point, mostly summers between sports.

Don kept his eye on business trends. He saw big box stores like Home Depot, Lowes, Walmart, and Menards were taking over the small lawn equipment businesses. They could purchase equipment for half of what Don could buy it and didn't offer service. Buyers were attracted by the prices and forgot about service.

Don was a visionary and an entrepreneur. He knew he needed to reinvent the business. Realizing there was an opportunity and market for larger equipment, he found the Kubota dealership available and seized the opportunity. He made a successful conversion, saved the business, and has been making record sales for the last few years.

The Dakin's story is one of success and achievement. Don, Mary, and John have worked together in their business for many years now. Mary has managed the office and kept the books, migrating to the company when her former employer, Jacobson's, closed their doors. The Dakins have taken pride in the service they have provided customers over the years. They raised their family from the business and have lived the American dream. I am proud to have been part of this thus success story begun by a great entrepreneur.

# CHAPTER 38:

## *Riviere-Koksoak, Quebec,*
## *September 2012*

My good friend Ed Machnik said I introduced him to big-game hunting. I am not so sure of that, but I do know he is hooked on the sport. At onetime Ed focused on NASCAR racing. He still loves racing but now he watches all the hunting shows on TV. And he continues to come up with ideas for exotic hunts we should take.

In September of 2011, Ed showed me pictures of a Caribou shot in northern Quebec with some impressive antlers. We heard from friends about their great hunting experiences near the Arctic Circle, so we checked sites on the internet, picked a few, and then interviewed each by phone. The outfitter we selected was based in Montreal. The company had two openings for late September at $5000 per person. The price included lodging for six nights, meals, a guide, and transportation from Montreal to the camp. We booked the hunt, made a substantial deposit, and discussed what ammunition, guns and clothing we would need.

I have fond memories of hunting in northern Michigan with my Uncle Gale Willis. His widow gave me his favorite gun after he died, a Winchester Model magnum. Each time I practiced shooting with that rifle I thought of him. He had the stock cut down to fit his short arms and body. The gun did not fit my body.

Coincidently, after my sister-in-law's dad and my brother Larry died, Barb gave me their guns including an identical match to Uncle Gale's Winchester 70-300 magnum. I took this rifle, some ammunition and tried it out on a 200-yard range Ed had set up. The 70-300 magnum fit fine but the shells hit the target inconsistently. Ed tried the gun and experienced the same result. When all the shells were spent we called it a day.

We applied for a permit to take our guns into Canada and registered with the U.S. Department of Customs and Immigration in Lansing, so we would not have a problem bringing them back. Luggage was limited to 50 pounds each. We carried our guns in special cases and had a carry-on backpack for clothes, hiking, knee-high and waterproof boots. We had to be ready for a temperature range of 10 to 50 degrees Fahrenheit, for rain, snow, and sun. After all, we were headed towards the Arctic tundra and the caribou migrating south.

I arrived at Ed's home in Michigan Center early on September 10, 2012. His gear was loaded, and we were off. It took patience for the eight-hour drive to Montreal. We met a couple of hunters at our hotel who were also heading to the Artic. They joined us for a dinner before we all hit the sack. At sunrise we met our outfitter and were shuttled to the airport. We joined a group of longbow hunters from Adrian and Monroe, Michigan. We all boarded the Boeing 737 filled with huntsmen and natives of the northern villages for the 900-mile flight to a small town established by Native Americans centuries ago.

At the village we were directed to another staging area to meet the other twelve hunters going to our camp. We realized this would be a new experience but were still surprised when we learned none of them spoke English. There were ten French Canadians from Montreal, two men from France, and Ed and me.

We boarded old seaplanes that could land on water or on flat spots on the tundra. We traveled in one and the baggage was loaded in the second. The low altitude flight gave us a good visual of the terrain with lakes, scrub brush, and rocky soil covered with moss.

When the planes finally circled the camp, I could see one small, solid strip of land with milk jugs tied to the ground to mark the landing strip. I said to Ed, "Do you believe we are going to land there?" He was silent. Everyone on the plane was silent. We circled the area again and began our descent to the strip between the milk jugs. I reminded myself to be patient, said a quiet prayer and told myself these pilots must know what they are doing. We did hit the runway. We bounced three or four times and came to a stop. The plane pivoted and taxied to the other end of the strip while we zipped our jackets. The temperature outside was 35. We leaned into the 30 MPH wind, made our way to a shelter, and waited for ATVs with trailers to take us to the camp on the edge of two wilderness lakes.

Ed and I were assigned to a cabin for six people. Two Frenchmen and two men from Montreal joined us. Our cabin was simple to say the least. A propane-heating stove stood at one end. Three cots lined each side. Nails and hooks on the walls were there to hang our clothes. Previous hunters had written on the walls bragging of their successes. They noted the size of the caribou, the number of fish taken, and the number of ptarmigan birds harvested including the dates they hunted.

After we arranged our gear we walked outside to scope out the grounds and were approached by one of the two guides who spoke French and English. He directed us to the two outhouses to show us the simple showers with limited heaters. We saw three other small cabins and learned two were for guests and one was for the guides. The man took us to the "dining room," a small hut where we would have our meals. The camp electricity was provided with a generator fueled with propane.

The other hunters retrieved their rifles and started target practice. They waved us over with a smile and motioned for us to join in. Their offer of friendship turned out to be the key to my hunting success. We pulled our guns from the cases, grabbed our shells, and headed for the range. I shot Uncle Gale's look-alike Winchester several times at 100 meters and failed to hit the target. Ed fired a couple of shells and hit the bullseye. They pulled the target closer for me. At 50 meters I still missed.

I was growing impatient and began to panic because I had a firearm with a scope that could not hit the broad side of a barn! There was no way I could shoot a caribou with this gun and now I was down to one box of shells. The Canadians came over and looked at my rifle. They noticed the sight had been improperly installed. With each shot it would move and be out of alignment. They retrieved some tools from their cabin and corrected the problem. I fired six more shells and was now sited in.

The new challenge was that I had only six shells left to start the big game hunt and my contract included licenses for two caribou. A check of guns in camp revealed there were no others with comparable ammunition.

We went outside to enjoy the sunset and used our binoculars to scan the rolling landscape for caribou. Members of the group shouted and pointed to small moving dots on the horizon. There were caribou in every direction more than a mile away.

The dinner bell rang, and we quickly gathered, carrying our own beer or wine that had been flown in with us. We sat at a table with the two Frenchmen. It seemed we used more hand signals than we did conversation. The camp cook came to our table taking orders. To our pleasant surprise, she spoke only English. The menu was simple, and we quickly found out how much English the French and French Canadians could speak. Survival can bring out creative language skills.

Back at the cabin we prepared for the early morning hunt. We laid everything out for easy dressing. We would not return to camp until dusk the next evening. Our cabin's small fuel oil heater was inadequate, so we crawled inside our zero-temperature sleeping bags when it was still daylight outside.

I awoke about four hours later for my midnight restroom call, exiting the cabin into the cold night. I was surprised to see the amount of daylight and quickly realized the sky was heavily influenced by the Northern Lights. It should not have been a large surprise as we were less than 100 miles from the Arctic Circle.

Our cabin came to life about four in the morning. We dressed, devoured our breakfast in the dining hut and picked up our boxed lunches. The two guides gave each party of two hunters the direction we were to head from camp: north, northeast, and east, and so on around the compass. Ed and I headed west across the airport landing strip. We had no guide that day and were armed with only a general idea on how to hunt these animals. It felt like the wind was blowing 40 miles an hour. We had to walk at a 45 degree angle through a light snow to penetrate the wind until we found the shed at the airport to hide behind to catch our breaths. We trudged on for at least three miles before we came to an area with rolling hills lined with some low scrub brush on the wet tundra. We sat there for an hour before deciding to move on.

When noon approached, we stopped for lunch. We sat on the ground to enjoy our food and discuss our strategy for the afternoon. We had not seen a single caribou all morning and were growing impatient. We continued our hunting strategy of walking and hiding in the afternoon. Surrounded by 200-foot rocky elevations, we were not afraid of getting lost. If we could see the lake through our binoculars, we would see the camp, both a long walk away.

Ed and I began to have a difference of opinion on how to hunt these animals. So, Ed went in his direction and I in another. The day moved on without a sighting. I glassed the horizon and located the camp that was now miles away. I selected the shortest route to camp, which turned out to be the most difficult walk of my life.

I crossed elevated terrain lined with grass and rock. The lowland walking was strenuous. I carried 30-40 pounds of gear through shallow water, grass and bogs. Although I had conditioned myself, I now realized I was not as young as I used to be. I scanned the horizon looking for one of the camp's ATVs to come and rescue me. No one came. I trudged on.

The camp went in and out of sight as I climbed hills and dropped into gullies. It seemed like I was making little progress. I reached a lowlevel panic and pushed myself more than I should have. I was in a heavy sweat. My heart was pounding. I kept moving. I considered myself to be in good shape and wondered how the others were surviving this terrain. I marveled at why we hunters put ourselves in situations like this. It was supposed to be fun and a vacation.

I finally reached the camp and consumed a couple of bottles of water. I was exhausted. Ed arrived soon after me in the same condition. We grabbed a semi-hot shower, quick dinner, and went to bed. We both agreed the day had been quite an experience.

The weather improved with each day and we learned how to handle the tundra. It was our turn for a guide in day three. Ed shot his first caribou. I did not care if I bagged a caribou, but if I did, I wanted to take the right one. I would be patient and wait for a large rack. When the guide positioned me for a decent shot, I took a bull down with one shot.

I was satisfied with my game while Ed and the others continued to hunt and bag their second caribou. I tagged along with Ed and a guide on day five. The guide drove an ATV, so we could ride part of the trip. Now this was the way to hunt! We positioned ourselves on top of a hill and glassed for trophy antlers. We saw thousands of caribou migrating south and feeding on choice grasses and moss. We were in the perfect camp and location for hunting.

Through our binoculars on the hilltop we spotted a nice bull. The range finder said it was 500 yards away, more than a quarter of a mile. Ed received permission from the guide to shoot. Ed will always try the impossible. He fired and missed, fired and hit, fired and missed, and finally downed the bull with the fourth shot. The guide dressed out the animal. The meat would be processed for us to take home along with the antlers and cape. There would be no waste at this camp.

The hunting was spectacular. Fourteen of the fifteen hunters filled both of their licenses. I carried the only unfilled license. The lead guide encouraged me to hunt with him that last day. It was hard to turn down the lead guide and an ATV. His motivation was to get a big tip and mine was to shoot the largest caribou. I agreed with the caveat that I would only take my shot if it would be the largest bull harvested by our camp. It would be an awesome day whether I shot a caribou or not.

We watched thousands of caribou on that clear morning. We stopped for a box lunch and talked about our families and other hunts. As we continued our search of the horizon the guide motioned for me to get in the ATV. He pointed to an area at least a mile away and a herd moving southeast.

Anticipating their movement, we drove toward a point ahead of the herd. We cleared hills and wetlands, staying out of sight. We stopped near the converging point. The guide and I jumped from the ATV and headed behind a hill on a dead run. The guide slowed from time to time, waving me on. He was young. I was breathing hard, anticipating the instant I would see the large bull. Three large bulls appeared in the opening between the hills and gazed down at us. My every sense was alert. They must have been a hundred yards away.

The guide told me to shoot in anticipation of their movement. I sat on the ground, released the safety, and laid the Winchester on my knee. The adrenalin flowed. I took a quick shot. I had never practiced a shot like that in my life.

The bull did not go down. I thought I missed, but the guide smiled as he looked down at me. He told me to put my rifle down. He saw the wound through his binoculars and said it was a perfect shot. I sat there relieved as I caught my breath. I never cease to be amazed at the talent of a professional guide.

The huge caribou dropped to the ground a few seconds later. I stood and enjoyed the slow walk to the bull. It was clear this was the largest animal taken in our camp. We took pictures as I admired the magnificent animal. It's times like these when patience is a lucky virtue.

The big one that didn't get away. Quebec 2012.

# CHAPTER 39:

## *Staying Power*

It's easier to build a business than to maintain it at the top, and rare for a company to survive beyond the second generation. I have had the opportunity to work with three generations of 15 to 20 Michigan families over my career as a business and tax advisor. I have mentored my original client's children and grandchildren, guiding them to continue making improvements within the focus of their business.

One of my favorite and most unique client experiences is the Jonesville Lumber Company. I remember my first trip there in December 1967 with Robert Campbell soon after I bought into his CPA firm. Bob's tradition was to leave from home early, have breakfast in a local Jonesville restaurant where he planned his work, and be off to the client by 8 a.m. Bob introduced me to Clyde Graves, an older gentleman who owned Jonesville Lumber. Clyde's father started the lumberyard around 1900. I met Clyde's son, Donald.

The Graves family managed the business meticulously, overseeing every transaction. They made sure each customer knew they cared about their business. The books were maintained in neatly written journals and ledgers listing every customer transaction. The entries were totaled for each month and carefully posted to the general ledger. A trial balance was run to prove that all was in balance, and a financial statement was prepared monthly. Clyde knew and understood where they stood in their finances each and every day. Their accounting yearend was November 30.

Our job was to perform an analytical evaluation, prepare a financial statement and the income tax returns in accordance with generally accepted accounting standards. We spent the entire day at their office, leaving them with numbers to determine year-end bonuses, and completed the work back at our office. Later we met to make recommendations and obtain signatures on tax returns. We delivered year-around service by meeting in the winter for personal tax services and by communicating by telephone and letters.

Years passed, and Clyde sold the business to the third generation of the Graves family. Donald had the youth, foresight, and entrepreneurial spirit to acquire the land and building across the street. Someday he could build a larger, more modern facility to service customer needs. His vision expanded. He bought adjoining land with a rail bed that had a potential for rail shipments and truck transportation. His son Jim was now working in the yard where materials arrived, were stacked, and later sold to customers. Jim was learning the business like his dad had, from the ground up. He could visualize every piece of material, learned lumber terminology, and served customers so he would better understand their needs and preferences.

Donald called me one day, asking to meet. He came to my office and explained that he had been diagnosed with a terminal disease and that he had about five years to live. Then a young man in his early 50s, he said he needed to transition the business to his son, Jim.

We designed a plan that met each party's goals. It called for installment payments to benefit Don and his wife for 20 years. This was a large commitment for Jim, but he assumed the debt in a positive spirit with no hesitation. The business had been there for 70 years and certainly could survive 20 more. Jim quickly moved to the office side of the business and underwent a crash course in management. Donald felt Jim was ready to take over and retired to enjoy his last few years.

Timing was not in Jim's favor. Shortly after he took over the business, the State of Michigan entered the recession. Great management and a conservative fiscal lifestyle allowed the company to survive when more than 50% of their competitors closed during the next few years. Jonesville Lumber Company survived because Jim decided to make huge investments in equipment, service, delivery systems, and technology. He made their company a leader in the industry.

The blessing of this potential tragedy is that Donald was misdiagnosed or received some treatments that cured his terminal disease. The father and son recently celebrated the final payment of the 20 year debt payment schedule. Donald is now living to see his grandchildren in the business!

I can generally tell if the next generation is prepared and has the mental capability to take over for the future of a business. Jonesville Lumber is poised for success over the next 30 years. Ben, Abe, Jim, Jolie and their two sons are hard workers with the same passion of their ancestors. I am impressed with their patience and excellent listening skills. They have a great opportunity to take over a successful business, to carry on the tradition, and to make themselves and their ancestors proud.

By the same token, these young men cannot rest on the laurels of their forefathers. Instead of following the same patterns of success of previous generations, they will need to study and monitor changing trends as world conditions evolve. They will have to "get out of the box," and not be afraid to make changes and take risks. They will need to meet with their peers, competitors, and business advisors. They must never stop asking questions and listening to the thoughts of others.

Jim Graves called me out of the blue this year. He said, "I was just thinking about you. We need to get together for dinner some night soon. Let me know when you return from Florida and we will set a date. I think I owe you a meal." This mutual respect builds relationships with the next generation, young folks who will continue to build successful family businesses and carry on the tradition of their ancestors.

# CHAPTER 40:

## The Incident; Farewell TransAction

We departed from Key West on *TransAction* with our friends Diane and Barron Clemons. It was the beginning of May of 2016. Our heading was Miami. This was another one of the hundreds of adventures we had enjoyed with friends since we bought the vessel 16 years ago. It was a perfect day for boating. We cruised for about four hours and stopped for a snorkeling break at the Hen and Chickens reef outside of Islamarada. We were in no hurry, had lunch, and after an hour or so of enjoying the sea we started for Miami.

The vessel was running smoothly, and everything seemed to be normal up on the bridge when we all heard a loud bang coming from below. I checked the salon. Smoke. I did a quick look inside the engine room. It was filled with smoke too. "We have a problem," I told the crew calmly when I came topside. As I checked our coordinates I was concerned about my passenger's safety. I had seen pictures of burning vessels before and knew how fast a fire could expand. *TransAction* was near marker 32a on the Intercostal Waterway. I knew our crew was comfortable around water and would be prepared to jump. I instructed them to unload the dinghy and prepare to abandon ship.

While the crew unloaded the dinghy into the sea I made the call on our VHF radio that I never thought I would have to make. I called a MAYDAY.

Each of us grabbed life vests and one small satchel and climbed off *TransAction*. I pocketed a handheld radio and a GPS. We heard the Halon fire system engage to put out the fire in the engine room.

"Where's Pat?" I called to the crew standing next to me in the dinghy. That's when I learned my wife had climbed back aboard and gone below. Just as I was about to go after her she appeared on deck with her case of jewelry, and with a big smile, jumped into the dinghy.

Several vessels and a towing service had heard our Mayday call and circled the smoking *TransAction* to see that we were okay. We were floating in the dinghy not far away. A second towboat and the US Fish & Game rescue boat arrived. After three hours the smoke subsided, and the towboat suggested the vessel be towed into the Key Largo area. The professionals and I climbed aboard and checked the inside. It was uninhabitable but was safe enough for us to ride aboard on the bridge during the tow. I knew the vessel had to go to Miami, so I asked them to take us to the Miamarina.

We lived what I have learned over the years: "Do not worry about things you cannot control." We enjoyed the sunset and sipped wine all the way to Miami while under tow. After an eight hour journey behind Towboat U.S., we tied *TransAction* to its mooring in slip 32b and checked into the Courtyard Inn. We were all tired. It was around one the next morning.

A short sleep and hurried breakfast later we rented a car from Hertz and drove to the marina. I met with the personnel at the facility on the status of *TransAction* and told them of our plans. We gathered a few of our personal belongings from the blackened cruiser and drove to our condo in Bonita Springs. Months later I began looking for another vessel. Pat and I both knew from our years working in the business world that setbacks happen to everyone. We have replaced *TransAction* and our adventures at sea continue on our new vessel, *Prospector*.

# CHAPTER 41:

## *Holiday Campground, LLC*

The year was 2006 and the economy was on an expansive roar. New homes were going up everywhere in Jackson Country inflated by cheap money and fraudulent loans. The price of real estate had more than doubled in five years. It was time to dream.

The All Seasons Resort Campground lay a little more than a mile north of our farm oasis on Willis Road. It was positioned on 150 acres of rolling wooded land. Our family owned a 120 acre parcel that L shaped around a major portion of the campground. This parcel was our prime hunting preserve. My interest in the property was being able to control future development next to our land. I had no idea how to run a campground and I could see it would take mechanical knowledge I did not have.

Research confirmed the campground was part of a national membership organization with financial problems and a series of bankruptcies. It had managed to avoid paying 12 years of property taxes, more than $600,000, and was under the control of the Jackson County Treasurer. They also owed the IRS $12,000,000 and were under the control of the US Department of

Justice, the DOJ. The property was finally cleared for sale from the bankruptcy court and was placed on the auction block with the DOJ managing the sale.

I saw opportunity. I talked with our good friends, Ed and Marie Machnik, about a partnership. Ed is an idea guy with a world of knowledge about maintenance and construction. Sorting his great ideas from his other fresh ideas is a frequent exercise for me. Ed and Marie completed their due diligence, were satisfied the campground had potential, and we agreed to become partners. We formed the Holiday Campgrounds LLC and entered the bidding with the DOJ.

Several buyers started the bidding. All but one dropped out soon. He was a serious buyer and pushed the price up to the maximum we had agreed to pay. We stepped back, evaluated the property again and agreed the price per acre appeared realistic compared with recent values. Ed and I raised our number a couple more times and finally bought the campground. The property closing was in 30 days with Jackson County's treasury receiving most of the funds to offset delinquent property taxes and the DOJ getting the rest.

Now the work would begin. We would be rebuilding a rundown 120 site campground with only four paying customers. This Jackson County site was a double money pit with its shabby appearance and lack of capital.

The main campground entrance is off I-94, an interstate highway that runs between Detroit and Chicago. The 150-acre campground was a vacationer's destination, a nature and wildlife paradise. The area was jammed with golf courses, lakes, rivers and thousands of acres of State land. Potential was written all over the property.

Our vision was gradually to restore and upgrade all the buildings and facilities. We would make improvements every year by adding investment capital without touching cash flow.

Ed had large road building equipment, a 12-yard dump, a road grader, an excavator, and backhoes. He liked to putter. The project was a grown man's sandbox. My partner began by removing several old buildings, improving the power, water and sewers, hiring a painter to freshen the buildings and improving the roads and sites with crushed concrete and asphalt. The old place was beginning to take shape.

Three years passed. Business was improving but not meeting our expectations. Ed and I took a Saturday afternoon to check out the competition. We toured several campgrounds including the highly respected State of Michigan campground at Portage Lake, just five miles from us. We gathered their literature. One owner working on site was glad to talk with us, that is, after we purchased an ice cream cone. Ed and I had a new marketing vision by the end of that day.

Our current customer focus was on transient campers, short term stays. We were at capacity during the three, summer holiday weekends but low occupancy the rest of the season. We knew we could not carry the overhead on the transient business alone. Instead, we had to target a different customer base, seasonal campers who rent for the year.

We cut our seasonal rates nearly in half positioning us well below our competitors. We promoted the new rate at the Novi Camper Show in February. We advised our existing customers of their reduced costs, printed new brochures and posted the rates on our website. The word spread, and new business rolled in.

We planned to raise the reduced rates by $100 per season until the numbers were restored to market. That rate would be determined by that old economic theory of supply and demand. The price adjustment would not have worked if we, the investors, did not have more money to invest. We understood annual capital calls would be necessary to build the business.

Holiday Campgrounds was soon open from April through October. Customers stored campers on site for the winter. The transient business drew new prospects for future seasonal customers, but those campers still perceived the campground as being old.

Our next step was to expand the number of campsites to a remote area of old tent sites on wooded land. The plan to develop 34 new campsites with water, and 50 amp electric and sewer service would require long term planning and an engineer.

During the process of getting permits for plumbing and electrical from the State of Michigan DEQ, the

County Health Department and the Township, we ran into three governmental units with different requirements to do the same thing. My partner, Ed Machnik, sorted that out.

Our son, Scott Willis, was put in charge of construction. He had not taken a high level of interest in the campgrounds since the purchase but did handle maintenance projects. Construction work would take more money, time and effort and over a year to complete. Scott, and his wife Kris, bought a new camper and took up part time summer residency in the new section. My vision was that over time they would take over the camp management and operations. Their pride, enthusiasm and ideas for the business should make the campground even more successful. Kris and Scott became the camp managers in the summer of 2017.

We posted the new sites accepting reservations based on a seniority system. The demand was surprisingly good since new rates were considerably higher. Current and new campers quickly reserved most of the new campsites. The expansion had raised the perception of Holiday Campgrounds several notches and our revenue almost doubled the following year.

In 2016 Ed and I toured the same campgrounds we toured several years earlier including the State of Michigan camp. We were surprised to see our competitors standing still. Our camp had become the best in the area. We were working on even more improvements funded by operating cash instead of capital calls from investors.

Improvements completed in 2017 were the free WIFI access, the 26 new sites around Holiday Lake, and the replacing of the old swimming pool with a new pool.

We attribute the success of Holiday Campground to many of the business development theories and strategies that started in 1862 on Willis Road by my great grandfather. We used my father's hunting lessons again and again. My research and planning revealed we would need partners with business expertise, equipment, ideas and capital to turn this rundown campground around. We set the maximum price we were willing to pay and didn't go over that by much. Preparation involved market research before and during construction, while we were upgrading the existing buildings and campsites and during the construction of the additional sites. We hired good people to construct and manage the campground. We used cash flow instead of additional investor capital. The prize at the end of this hunt was the satisfaction that we had taken a simple business, added good people, ideas, and capital, and with perseverance, turned a failing campground into one with the best camping sites in Michigan.

Photo by Marcia Butterfield

Holiday Campground

# CHAPTER 42:

## *Perseverance: Key to Success in Building a Business*

I planned to conclude this book with ten bullet points that would outline the short course to success. I began my list, adding an item or two each time I sat down to write. When the list became unwieldy I realized my plan had a flaw. The secret to starting and maintaining a successful business lies in building a large inventory of ideas and then applying the best for the situation at hand. It is the decision-making process that counts. Here are just a few thoughts for your consideration:

1. Make decisions based on achieving long-term positive results.
2. Take emotion out of the decision-making process.
3. Work toward constant improvement. Success does not happen by accident.
4. Build confidence in yourself and in your team.
5. Lead by example. Let your actions do the talking.
6. Prepare long and short-term goals and to-do lists. Tackle the difficult and most important first.
7. Utilize the "cost verses benefit" strategy in making decisions.

8. Position yourself to take advantage of and seize opportunities.
9. Make hay while the sun shines
10. Plan and prepare. Aim for the target before you shoot the gun.
11. Good planning and management will achieve more than merely hard work.
12. Turn problems and challenges into opportunities.
13. Take risks and do not be afraid to make mistakes. Be an entrepreneur.
14. Remember, there is no letter "I" in the word TEAM.
15. Exercise patience. It takes time to build a business or complete a project.
16. Do not worry about things you cannot control.
17. Dream to exceed your expectations.
18. Be a good listener.
19. Believe in yourself and in your ideas.
20. Ask for the business. Follow up. Close the sale.
21. Do not become married to poor investments or employees.
22. Learn how to manage and avoid stress.
23. And, persevere in whatever you choose to do.

# CHAPTER 43

## *Drive Right Venture*

Venture capital is about investing money in an early phase or start up business or idea. I refer to my investments in non-public stock companies as private equity investing. I prefer purchasing a business with a track record with future potential for growth and improved profitability. Our goal is to generate great cash flow and build goodwill or intrinsic value. It takes focus, good people, perseverance and generally the investment of more capital.

A long-term client advised me that he and his partner wanted to close their business, liquidate their assets and retire. The business imported right hand drive Jeeps, performed major rebuilds and sold them to US Postal carriers. Many carriers today furnish their own vehicles and are paid mileage by the government. The business is a complicated operation regulated by layers of governmental red tape.

I had been their CPA and financial consultant for many years and told them that I believed that the operation had goodwill value and they should try to sell.

They contracted me to assemble an offering memorandum. I presented a draft a week later. We fine-tuned the memorandum and both parties began the search for a buyer. I dropped off a memorandum to our son and asked if he had any potential buyers. I said it was a good business with potential.

A week later he said, "Why don't we buy the business?" I responded by saying that we are not purchasing any more businesses. I had no intention of purchasing the business and flat out told him so. Go find someone else in your business circle that may be interested. Dan was a partner in a flourishing financial adviser firm with his mother and my wife, Pat. I presented the opportunity to a few people and associates at the CPA firm. No interest. I spoke with Dan and he had no prospects.

He replied, "Why don't we buy it!".

"No way are we purchasing another business. We did not have the team or expertise to run it." We were having lunch with a group of hunting buddies at a local Grass Lake pub when it hit us both at the same time. The key person eating a hamburger at the end of the table was the missing link to this business venture.

Craig Deck was working at an automotive testing lab and possessed mechanical and management skills.

Dan and I spoke later and decided to ask Craig Deck if he would be interested. He was a long-term family friend. I was beginning to change my mind and thought it would be great experience for Dan. The experience would provide a succession plan for our other family ventures. Dan has seen some of the successes and was ready to enter the private equity business. I made it clear to him that he could not lose focus on his core business as an investment adviser, Golden Goose.

Craig said he would join the team. Family discussions were held and Pat decided to invest with us. It was a substantial capital investment. My son had changed my mind!

We knew the right team would be a necessity for long-term success. We added another valuable member, my long term administrative assistant, Darlene Scouten and a seasoned sales person, Julie Wortman. We have struggled at times but we keep pushing to evolve the business into a successful venture. Dan, wife Angela and daughter Olivia, have entered the private equity business. Dan is keeping his focus on his core business and doing a great job of maneuvering through the government regulations.

This business is a work in progress!

# CHAPTER 44:

## *My Legacy*

My goal in life was never to be wealthy. I just wanted to be the best that I could be at whatever I did. I looked for opportunities, did my due diligence and then turned the opportunities into successes using lessons I learned duck hunting with my father. As I look back at my contribution to what will be of value to future generations, I can sum it up in one statement: I did my share and a little bit more. I led a talented team of accountants to help families, associations, and the Jackson community to develop and manage their businesses. I led organizations that helped the economy in Michigan recover from the 1980's recession.

I credit much of my leadership success to enhancing the lives of others. I find good people, establish entrepreneurial centers and empower them to make decisions. Their rewards are based on results. My job as a leader is to monitor and enhance their performance, let them lead and then stay out of the way.

My efforts have provided jobs in Jackson County. Thirty-five of the business startups from BIDCO and the Venture Capital Group were successful. I have carried forward Willis family traditions putting family first, holding on to family lands, preserving nature and protecting wildlife. I have organized and led groups of volunteers to preserve the historic Whistlestop Train Station and the Lost Railway Museum. I have mentored my own children and grandchildren by my example in giving back to the communities where we live.

Little comes easily for me. I must work at it. For example, this book has taken over four years and many revisions. Writing *TransAction* took a huge commitment of my time and energy but completing it has given me a great deal of satisfaction. While writing I recalled the long history of positive events in my life. The process frequently offered me a different perspective on life and on the things, I have done. It opened my eyes and mind to new ideas, many of which I utilize in my daily routine. I still would rather make history than write about it. But who knows, I may take another book-writing break one of these days.

Pat and I are living the results of our hard work and investments but have no plans to retire. We spend time with family and friends and remain involved with our community. We enjoy our Florida home and boat as well as our beautiful lake home in Jackson. We look forward to traveling and plan trips both in this country and abroad.

Remaining active in our businesses and community rewards us at the end of each day. We thrive on our consulting and volunteer activities while enhancing the lives of others.

We worked and invested well. We enjoy each day and can live the lifestyle we desire. We have taught our children and grandchildren financial responsibility and have encouraged them to find something they love to do for a living. Most of our family members have worked for me during summer vacations and after graduation, doing everything from yard work around my office property to other tasks. I have asked each one to send me an invoice to get paid. I love sharing life and business philosophies with them.

I am a grateful man. I have had my share of failure. I have learned from my mistakes. All in all, I have had more hits than misses. I have helped others achieve their financial goals and have been the CPA for generations of many of my clients. If this book can help share what I have learned in a way that inspires others to take control of their financial lives, to work toward good health, and to get involved in their communities, then my job is done, and this project has been a worthwhile effort. If all you take away from my story is to do your share and little bit more, then I believe you will increase your success and satisfaction in life.

Check in with yourself from time to time; ask yourself if you are enjoying your life. If the answer is no, or not really, see what you can change or do to enhance your quality of life. Set new goals to work toward. It's your life and in the end, no one is responsible for your joy but you. Ultimately, fulfillment comes from the relationships you have had, the lives you have helped change, and the happy memories you can review whenever you want to. All of those are so much more valuable than the balance in your bank account.

Thank you for reading my story – and here's to your success!

The End

Sesquicentennial family reunion

Scott Willis, Phil Willis Jr., Dan Machnik, and me enjoying time with my three sons.

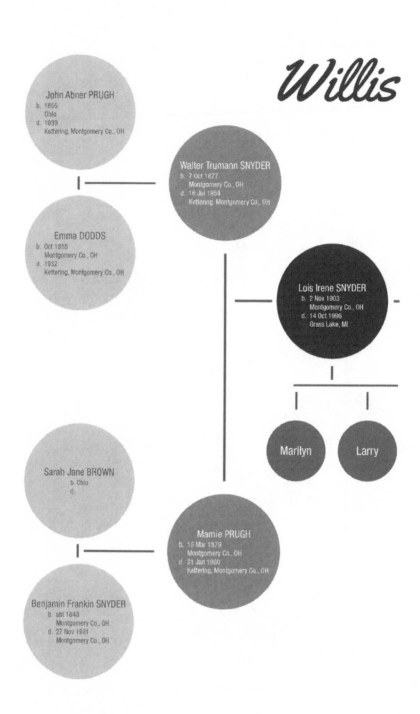

*Willis*

John Abner PRUGH
b. 1855
Ohio
d. 1939
Kettering, Montgomery Co., OH

Walter Trumann SNYDER
b. 7 Oct 1877
Montgomery Co., OH
d. 16 Jul 1954
Kettering, Montgomery Co., OH

Emma DODDS
b. Oct 1855
Montgomery Co., OH
d. 1932
Kettering, Montgomery Co., OH

Lois Irene SNYDER
b. 2 Nov 1903
Montgomery Co., OH
d. 14 Oct 1996
Grass Lake, MI

Marilyn

Larry

Sarah Jane BROWN
b. Ohio
d.

Mamie PRUGH
b. 15 Mar 1879
Montgomery Co., OH
d. 31 Jan 1960
Kettering, Montgomery Co., OH

Benjamin Frankin SNYDER
b. abt 1848
Montgomery Co., OH
d. 27 Nov 1931
Montgomery Co., OH

# Family

**George (Dr.) WILLIS**
b. 21 Jan 1829
Meigs, Cayuga Co., NY
d. 6 Jan 1894
Jackson, Jackson Co., MI

**Phil Sheridan WILLIS ('Sherd')**
b. 17 Sept 1867
Plymouth Twp., Wayne Co., MI
d. 20 Feb 1936
Grass Lake, Jackson Co., MI

**Helen E. JONES**
b. 9 Feb 1834
New York
d. 18 Sep 1920
Jackson, Jackson Co., MI

**Phil Sterling WILLIS**
b. 28 Nov 1902
Grass Lake, MI
d. 16 July 1962
Grass Lake, MI

**Grace**

**Phil**

**Ester Jane WOODIN**
b. 13 Mar 1840
Half Moon, Saratoga Co., NY
d. 26 Apr 1902
Jackson Co., MI

**Sarah J. TAYLOR**
b. 15 May 1867
Grass Lake, Jackson Co., MI
d. 1940
Grass Lake, Jackson Co., MI

**Joel Clay TAYLOR**
b. 17 Feb 1823
New York
d. 29 May, 1876
Grass Lake, Jackson Co., MI

265

# ABOUT THE AUTHOR

Besides being an entrepreneur, businessman, and recipient of numerous local, national, and association awards, including Michigan CPA Volunteer Award, Michigan Small Business Employer Award, and National SBA Accountant Advocate for Small Business Award, the author is a husband, father, and grandfather. Lifetime residents of Michigan, he and his wife, Pat, make their home in Jackson, Michigan.